Transformational
LIVING

From Emotional Pain to Happiness

DR. JOHN

Gotham Books

30 N Gould St.
Ste. 20820, Sheridan, WY 82801
https://gothambooksinc.com/

Phone: 1 (307) 464-7800

© 2025 *Dr. John*. All rights reserved.

No part of this book may be reproduced, stored in a retrieval system, or transmitted by any means without the written permission of the author.

Published by Gotham Books (March 12, 2025)

ISBN: 979-8-3485-1772-4 (H)
ISBN: 979-8-3485-1770-0 (P)
ISBN: 979-8-3485-1771-7 (E)

Because of the dynamic nature of the Internet, any web addresses or links contained in this book may have changed since publication and may no longer be valid.

The views expressed in this work are solely those of the author and do not necessarily reflect the views of the publisher, and the publisher hereby disclaims any responsibility for them.

Table of Contents

Understanding Essence 1
The Four Basic Points of Connection 29
Understanding Attachment 41
What Goes Wrong During the Attachment Process? 97
Existential Aloneness 134
Grief and Loss: 145
Healing Our Wounds/Rewiring Our Internal Working Model 157
    Johns Trigger-Wound Exercise 168
    Anxiety's Tripod 176
    Cognitive Processing Flowchart 178
Becoming Proactive with Our Children 185
Understanding How Attachment is the Foundation of All Pathology 215
Attachment as a Sociological Disorder 239

1

Understanding Essence

We need to understand who we are before we understand our purpose in life, what perceptions are, and how others see us. We need this before we can really help our children grow into the adults God has intended them to become. Healthy people do not accept that life is something that happens to us, nor do they believe that life is something that happens while we are busy making other plans.

Self-Actualized individuals vomit at the idea that we are products of our environment. If any of the above statements are true, then atheists are correct in their thinking, and there is no purpose in our lives. We need to understand that we are designed on purpose, by purpose, and for purpose. We need to discover what our talents are and the characteristics which make up our unique personality.

The largest psychological debate for the past one hundred years has been nature (genetics) versus nurture (environment) although the debate ends up with the combination of the two being intertwined. We need to understand if that is all there is, then God has no part in our development. When we take on the challenging task that we are much more than monkeys (see and we do) and much more than just genetics and much more than the results of our parents; we move toward the major challenge in life and discover who we are and who we are designed to be. In order, to take on this challenge, we must explore the origin of our identity.

Where does our identity come from? Is our identity formed? If our identity is formed, then does the formation of our identity stop? Does trauma change us as is a common belief? Many individuals say they have changed from the person they were ten years or even five years ago.

The common belief amongst psychologists is that the personality is formed in the first six to seven years of life. If that is true, then do babies transform into completely different individuals than who they were when they were born. How much does our environment affect our identity?

Are individuals some type of unique life form that our identity is dependent upon our environment?

Does our identity create a predisposition to social problems, personality problems, addictions, anxiety, stress, depression, or to whether we marry, go to college, or become a millionaire? Is our identity connected to our behaviors or our beliefs? These are some of the questions we will ponder and address throughout this book.

There is something very unique about individuals, and that uniqueness to a variety of behaviors and emotional reactions is much deeper than just our environment or our genetic predisposition. The Bible states that Jesus knew us in the womb. Webster states that the word know means to be certain of, to perceive directly with the senses or mind, to possess knowledge, to be aware of, to possess correct or secret knowledge. There was no doubt in Jesus' mind who we are or who it is that we are to become.

He formed us with unity and with uniqueness. It is God who grants us our intelligence, our imagination, and all the gifts and talents we have inside of us. They are gifts granted to us to use to help others, to fulfill our purpose in life, to bring joy to our lives as well as to others. They are not gifts to lord over others or to boast in the true sense of the word.

There is nothing wrong when we express our gifts or give credit to the person who gave us our gifts.

When someone compliments you on a piece of jewelry you are wearing, you don't say Oh this old thing, it's nothing. Rather you smile and proudly mention that it was a gift and you mention the person whom gave it to you and express the love between you and your loved one whom gave you the gift. This is what I believe we are called to do with the gifts given to us from God. Boasting comes into play when we are bragging about what we have, and others do not or about what we have done ourselves. When we realize who gave us our inner gifts and we realize the purpose of the gifts as well as there is a unity with our Maker, we are living in our essence.

When we live in our essence, we know who we are, what our purpose is, and what we have to offer the world. When we live in our essence, we don t react to life out of our insecurities. We are not concerned with competition for competition's sake. We are not concerned with worldly recognition.

It is nice when it happens, and just as competing can be fun for those of us who are competitive, it is also temporary and can be addictive. When we live in our essence, we simply live. We are free to be ourselves and to be comfortable with ourselves. When we live out of our essence, there is nothing to prove to others. Yet all of us spend significant time wasted in attempting to prove ourselves and our beliefs about the world and ourselves to others.

We have bought a huge lie that this is going to give us security and bring us a belief that we are okay. The only two people who can give us the only true security we need is ourselves and God. When we live out of our essence, we do not live out of our insecurities and our defenses.

We simply are okay with who we are and just show up in the place that we need to be in that moment. Knowing our essence gives us our security because it is our essence that we have unity and security with God. It is our essence that gives us our security because there is nothing to defend. Animals do not defend out of identity; they defend out of survival.

When we live out of our essence, we are not surviving; we are thriving. We know with certainty that we have worth and that we will be taken care of. We may not receive from others or from the world what we had hoped for. We may not even receive from God what we had hoped for, but if we open our eyes, we do receive what is necessary. Since it is our essence that gives us our unity and security with God, then what is essence?

Does essence differ from personality? Webster defines personality as the state or quality of being a person with distinctive characteristics. Freud said Give me the boy up to age seven, and I will give you the man.

There are hundreds of theories, by many brilliant psychologists, on how the personality is formed. This book introduces to begin thinking about essence and personality. I strongly believe it is our essence, which comes from God, that makes us unique. Otherwise, we become exactly like everyone else who has grown up with similar circumstances.

We become more like a programmable robot dictated to behave according to our emotional environment. Or we are commended by our genes and there is no other choice to behave according to our genetic predisposition. Psychologists teach that individuals will have different reactions to the same incident or event based upon how an individual interprets the incident or event. Pertaining to genetics, most mothers will tell you that they understood the difference in their child's personality even as early as the womb. So, how does essence and personality play out their roles with each other?

First, we need to define essence and then understand its role in comparison to the personality. I define essence as the person God created, the individual we were always meant to become. All our talents, gifts, and abilities are within our essence, Temperament, defined as relatively consistent and basic dispositions inherit in the person that underlie and modulate the expression of activity, reactivity, emotionality, and sociability is a small part of our essence.

I define personality, from its root word persona, as the person we present to others. We present the person we believe we need to present to be accepted by others or protected from others. Many insecure male teenagers will learn to walk a certain way to be viewed by others as cool.

These teens are working hard at hiding their insecurities and fears of rejection or being looked down upon by others. Many individuals, women and men, of any age will act in particular ways to acquire acceptance and to be protected from harm from others. The challenge is that these behaviors do not demonstrate the individual's true personality.

Some of these behaviors come out of rebellious acts toward their parents' beliefs. Other behaviors may come out of an attempt to earn their parents' attention and respect. The well-known comedian Jerry Lewis worked hard his entire life at attempting to acquire his father's respect and love and still never received it. When our behaviors are motivated by attempting to acquire attention or attempting to prove ourselves, we are not living out of our essence. When we live out of our essence, our behaviors are motivated by our beliefs that drive us toward an authentic sense of self.

So, what makes it difficult for us to live out of our essence? All of us have endured at least one's significant trauma in our lives, usually during our childhood. I am not saying that all of us have endured abusive backgrounds or significant neglect. What I am saying is that every individual has endured a significantly negative event in our early lives that has created an emotional reaction of shame, doubt, helplessness, mistrust, sadness, fear, anxiety, or anger. It is a natural human response to enduring trauma to somehow cover it up, avoid it and to create methods that would prevent it from happening again.

So, how do I define emotional or psychological trauma? Emotional trauma used to be defined as abuse or neglect. Thanks to the work of Dr. Bessel van der Kolk and other psychologists who are experts in the area of trauma, we have expanded our definition and viewpoints on trauma.

I will define emotional trauma as anything that occurs in our environment that does not compute in our brains but needs to compute in order to make sense out of what has happened to us. Trauma is chronic stress within our bodies. Other examples of trauma besides abuse and neglect include being a victim to a natural disaster, divorce, being a child of divorce, loss and grief. Another way to view emotional trauma is any type of change that impacts our living or work environment, including our body, lifestyle, or emotional support system, that creates a negative impact upon our lives and leaves us in a negative mental mindset.

Some might say that trauma changes us. With the theory of essence, I do not believe that trauma changes us; rather that the impact of trauma is that it buries our essence and creates a false identity. It's like a tree where no matter what happens to the tree it does not change the essence of the tree. The tree might lose a branch, the trunk might even split, the tree might even burn; however, the essence of the tree remains constant.

Obviously, we are far more complex than a tree or any other living thing. When animals experience trauma, such as being exposed to its predator, it reestablishes its original composure of peace and immediately carries on the nature of business it was tending to before the trauma occurred. We have this human nature to believe that if we can make sense of an event, we are back in control, and if we are in control, we are safe, and it is this very process that keeps us stuck in our trauma. It is this process that creates a false identity.

We personalize much of our environment, believing that what happens to us is somehow connected to our identity. With that belief, it is not much of a stretch to become arrogant because good things and our accomplishments are a direct reflection of who we are rather than to be blessings from God. This belief also works when we are mistreated by others. We need to recognize that we have no control over how others treat us, feel about us, or think of us. Every individual has his or her own freewill and ability to arrive at his or her own conclusions about any person. However, it is human nature to personalize the actions of others toward us.

Since, we believe that we somehow caused another person to treat us in a particular manner; we also believe we have the ability to change how people treat us. Therefore, we change our actions and sometimes attempt to change ourselves in order to avoid being hurt or traumatized. And we refuse to live out of our essence because we believe it is not safe to do so. Not living out of our essence becomes the ultimate defense mechanism. The younger the child is when trauma occurs, the more these beliefs are formed in the subconscious part of the brain. The huge challenge then becomes a lost sense of self.

Trauma affects us deeply. It creates a false sense of self, a false self-identity. It rewires the brain in our perceptions, creating listening filters that is overly sensitive to anything that might sound hurtful or perceived in any negative manner. We see things differently. We hear things differently. We react to things differently.

With children, their innocence is robbed from them, and they are now on a road of survival or self-destruction. We believe, especially if we have a weak foundation, that if bad things happen to us, it's because we are bad or there's something wrong with us. Children have no other choice, due to their egocentric makeup, but to absorb their environment like a sponge. When bad things happen to children, they believe it is because they are bad people. Bad things happen to bad people and good things happen to good people. This is a belief that all of us have at some point in our lives and a belief that all of us must transcend from in order to heal from our past.

In order to move beyond our false beliefs that we are somehow responsible for how others mistreat us; we must understand how trauma changes our beliefs. Trauma opens our eyes to the evil in the world. We lose our innocence. We lose our naivete. We acquire knowledge of good and evil and view the world as much more dangerous than if we had not had trauma enter into our lives.

We act differently. Some individuals act more aggressive. Others act more withdrawn. We see others as mistrusting. We view ourselves with much less value than what we should. We often interact with others in a more defensive manner. We become far more cautious about who can be considered emotionally safe. Many psychologists, including myself, believe that it is these early childhood traumatic events that is the root of most marital issues, the root of our communication challenges, and the root for poor life choices. In spite that our thinking has evolved along with how we interact with the world; our essence is still there. Our essence is just buried under layers of the manifested behaviors of our trauma.

So, just like a cluttered closet where there might lie a treasure. Our treasure, our essence is buried underneath a bunch of rubble. Another gigantic challenge is that most of us have never looked into our personal closets of self-identity because we believe there is no treasure at the back of our personal closet. We believe the lie that our self-identity is only the stuff that we see and show others. Therefore, as time marches on, our false belief of who we are becomes more solidified into our thinking. Our actions and false beliefs become etched into our automatic responses and we live out of our false beliefs, never taking the time to clean out our personal closets and discover the treasure.

For many years, psychologists referred to acting out of these false beliefs as the false self. My personal view is that it is extremely significant for individuals to know their personal history when it comes to understanding how their false self came into creation or how their essence became buried in the back of their personal closet.

Another significant way to understand how trauma has buried our essence is through understanding that trauma also creates fragmentation in the brain. Does it mean that the brain literally is broken into pieces? No. Fragmentation refers to an individual's ability to stay focused, to listen to detail, problem-solve, communicate clearly, utilize logic, and to be creative.

Trauma can create many learning delays such as in language, reading, and mathematics. Trauma often stunts cognitive development, causing many educational delays in an individual's learning. Often, the way children deal with these learning delays manifested by trauma is through aggression, withdrawal, or avoidance such as skipping school. The way adults deal with these learning delays often includes substance abuse (drugs and alcohol), crime, hanging out with other troubled individuals, being underemployed or unemployed, crime, and dating or marrying victims or perpetrators of abuse. Other developmental delays caused by psychological trauma create delays in our emotional development.

Trauma impacts or rewires the limbic system part of the brain. The limbic system is where the amygdala is, and its purpose is to regulate our emotions. The limbic system is also where our dopamine neural pathways, the pleasure hormones, operate.

Trauma can create an exaggerated expression of emotions, anxiety, and emotional passion, such as demonstrated in individuals diagnosed with borderline personality disorder. Trauma can also significantly suppress emotions in individuals creating or demonstrating withdrawal. You might know of an individual who is brilliant and appears to have the emotions of a young child. You might know of someone who demonstrates a lot of empathy toward others but appears to lack logic and problem-solving skills. Many psychologists, including myself would agree that trauma lowers intelligence.

Hopefully, you are asking is it possible to reverse the damage that trauma has caused. That is the purpose of this book. First, we must understand what the problem is before we can fix the problem. The correct circuits must be rewired. I have often worked with children, whose teachers and parents have said that there is something wrong with the child's brain. I taught these same folks that there actually is nothing wrong with the child's cognitive (thinking part of the brain), but the child's emotions (limbic system) are mis-wired due to the trauma he or she has experienced.

Another way that survivors survive or live past their trauma is through suppressing their memories. There has been a ton of debate over memories of survivors versus false memories. This discussion is beyond the scope of this book. All I want the reader to understand is that the brain is very powerful and sometimes the brain will automatically shut down due to overload of information.

The brain is overwhelmed. Have you ever noticed how tired you are at the end of a stressful day? Now, imagine a series of weeks, months, a few years of consistent stress. We also choose to block things out that are too painful to deal with. Overtime, we simply forget what we have hidden in our personal closets. It comes to surface in other manifestations, such as not trusting, withdrawing, or being aggressive toward others.

It is vital for our well-being to examine our motives for our behaviors. It is through understanding our motives that we can begin to examine how our motives became manifested. One of the ultimate goals God has for all of us is to heal our emotional and psychological wounds and return to our essence.

A well-known psychologist, Maslow, believed people live according to a hierarchy of needs. In Maslow's hierarchy of needs, he taught that everyone has to acquire the very basic needs of food and shelter, in order in order to live. However, Maslow also examined that people who were the happiest and healthiest mentally and physically were individuals who were striving toward achieving their fullest potential. He called this being self-actualized. It has been my experience that God wants us to achieve our fullest potential. God wants us to become self-actualized and for this to happen, one must live out of his or her essence. It is our essence where our natural born talents lie, where our intelligence and desires match our goals and eventually our accomplishments.

It is our responsibility to seek the counseling we need in order to reunite with our essence. The earlier the trauma has taken place in our lives, the more work is going to be required in order for us to return to our essence. For example, when a child under the age of five years old is molested, the deeper the trauma.

This is for several reasons. First, our personality is being formed during the first six years of life. Second, it is during the first three years of life that most learning and development occurs. Third, the earlier the age of onset that trauma occurs, the more impactful the trauma becomes. Fourth, the trauma that occurs during the early years of development is more likely to be trauma caused by trusted caregivers. Fifth, the child is less likely to have a support system, especially if the support system is responsible for causing the trauma. Sixth, the child at this age is going to most likely blame him or herself for his or her own trauma and believe that it is their destiny to be treated in abusive manners. This often creates a long consistent pattern of self-abuse, being abused by others, addiction, and/or other self-defeating patterns. A good counselor/psychotherapist can assist an individual in healing from early childhood trauma and many counselors specialize in this specific topic.

It is work on the client's part to be dedicated to healing from his or her trauma and discover his or her essence. The therapist's job is to coach, direct, guide; but, only the client can do the healing. The therapist can show the client that he or she is living out of his or her false self. Remember, the false self is created to protect and seek approval from others. Sometimes, the false self that is created attempts to hide his or her true intelligence and talents by acting less intelligent and almost helpless. Other times, the false self that is created is a façade attempting to hide one's shame, doubt, and inabilities and this is the root of narcissism.

The saying, all you have to do is set your mind to it, is a flat out lie and a form of narcissism to believe that anyone of us is capable of doing anything. However, it is also a flat out lie to believe that a person is not capable of anything. Every single individual has value and is capable of doing what they were designed by God to do. This is what it means to live out of our essence.

Trauma manifests in ways that causes us to not live out of our essence. It is our internal beliefs about ourselves and the world that are manifested from our interpretations of the trauma that we have endured. The gigantic challenge is that beliefs are stored in our subconscious-mind and we act and react out of automatic pilot. We are not aware of our motives for our behaviors.

It is often that you hear even adults say that they do not know why they did what they did. Even, Apostle Paul stated that he did not understand why he does the very things he hates to do and does not do the things he knows are right to do. Another aspect of beliefs is that we are forced to behave in ways that fit into our schemas, the ways others describe us or even the diagnosis given to us by professionals.

Labels and diagnoses can be a dangerous obstacle in attempting to discover our essence. We can buy into diagnoses, whether it be ADHD, Borderline Personality Disorder, or Narcissistic Personality Disorder and use it as excuses for our behaviors, including our insensitivity to others. We can believe that our diagnosis is our essence and then we live out of our diagnosis.

Our essence once again becomes buried. One day, I was walking my girlfriend's dog in my backyard when I noticed what I thought was a weed. As I started to pull it up, I noticed that it was actually a beautiful rose bush that got knocked down, trampled on and entangled with weeds. Isn't that a beautiful metaphor of our lives, where a lot of our lives get entangled in weeds and either us or others are quick to get rid of all of it, including the essence. That beautiful rose bush just needed to be cleaned up, mended, and nurtured back to the life and purpose it was designed to give, expressing joy, love, and beauty.

Sometimes we miss the beauty in our own lives and other times we miss the beauty in the lives of others. One of the most important things we can do in life is to discover and live out of our essence. One of the greatest gifts we can give to others is to help them discover their essence. We are quick to dismiss either ourselves or others as simply miserable, depressed, a worrisome annoyance, etc.

It is imperative to always take into account that we are probably not seeing the entire picture. Trauma impacts every aspect of an individual's life. Trauma can also get locked in the body. Rape victims can walk and move as if their hips and pelvis areas of their bodies are locked or frozen in place.

Many traumatized individuals grow into adulthood with poor blood circulation, back problems, and sometimes pulmonary issues. Stress, especially chronic and consistent stress, is a foundational attribute to heart, pulmonary (lung), or blood clot conditions later in life. The body wears the stress that has been manifested by trauma. The body can only take so much stress before it manifests into illness. If we can learn to heal from trauma sooner in our lives, perhaps we can avoid these illnesses later in life.

It is also significant to address trauma as early as possible in order to avoid the damage that trauma causes our ability to listen to others carefully and to empathize.

Often, trauma stunts our emotional development and traumatized individuals view people in black and white terms, as either good or bad. A healthy adult can understand that all individuals make mistakes that all individuals have a good side and a bad side. The ability to see an individual as whole, the good, bad, the ugly, and the beautiful is called the ability to integrate. A healthy and emotionally mature adult understands and accepts that no one is perfect. A healthy and emotionally mature individual can accept that we are not our behavior and learns to criticize the behavior without criticizing the person. Therefore, encouraging others to discover and live out of their essence.

It may seem like a giant hurdle to get over when attempting to separate another person's behavior from who that person truly is. It requires significant patience, grace, and mercy. It also requires enough humility to recognize that we are individuals struggling and that we make mistakes daily. It requires humility to recognize our contradictions in how we treat others and sometimes ourselves. Sometimes we are hard on ourselves when it isn't necessary and at other times, we are hard on others showing no compassion nor empathy.

We are multifaceted individuals filled with contradictions. We even have different perceptions of the same place that we have been too according to whom we are with and according to our mood. There are areas of our life that we feel confident and there are other areas where we do everything to avoid. There are things that we enjoy and things that we don t enjoy. The same is true for people. There are some people where conversation comes easily and we can talk for hours and there are other individuals where our conversations are strained.

Trauma also creates our projections for us. Projection refers to taking parts of our emotional or intellectual self and placing them onto others. These projections can either be good or bad. For example, we might say that a certain person is highly intelligent when it is you not the other person who is highly intelligent. We might also say that we see that person is mean or dumb based upon our expectations and subconsciously (without awareness) view that individual in the same light the person who has hurt us.

I remember working with a client whose wife divorced him after he grew a beard. His beard created a projection on him from his wife that he was not trustworthy and hurtful. Her father who molested her had a beard. A young woman standing in line in McDonalds dropped some money. The older gentleman standing behind her picked it up and handed it to her. Later, she called the police and told them that this man attempted to rape her. These are extreme cases, but all of us project. It is just one way we attempt to defend our beliefs about ourselves and the world.

Another defense mechanism is our coping mechanisms. Coping mechanisms can be either good or bad and can include reading, work, drugs, alcohol, and sex. However, when we use our coping mechanisms to not feel, that is not good. While defense mechanisms are more characteristic attributes like withdrawal and aggression. Coping mechanisms are more behavioral traits like drugs, alcohol, sex, and work. We use both defense mechanisms and coping mechanisms to deal with our internal emotional pain.

One difference is that coping mechanisms are more blatant. Coping mechanisms are external behaviors, which the individual believes will help them cope with their uncomfortable emotions, thoughts, and perceptions. We feel an uncomfortable emotion or attempting to deal with stress and anxiety through some quick fix to avoid feeling these uncomfortable feelings. We need to address our pain by first acknowledging our pain. We also need to understand the root of emotions and understand where this particular emotion is coming from.

Understanding the root of emotions and our thought processes can involve some hard, challenging work. It involves acquiring insight as well as the willingness to look at our lives as well as the significant people (parents, spouses, relatives) and their actions toward us. We must examine our reactions to the actions of others. Our emotions are often linked to our interpretations and our interpretations are often linked to our past experiences.

Some examples of how our emotions are linked to interpretations, which is linked to our past can include individuals who were abused by their parents or individuals who were rejected by their parents. Individuals who were abused by their parents often grow up to be adults who struggle with depression and/or anxiety. In addition, the individual with an abusive background can become a very mistrusting adult and respond to others either with withdrawal or aggression as well as struggle with low self-esteem. Individuals who were rejected by their families as children, either through neglect, emotional abuse, or abandonment also struggle with low self-esteem, depression, and anxiety.

It can be more challenging to heal from neglect than abuse because we can see abuse and there are specific events that are linked to abuse. Neglect, on the other hand, is often not always obvious or visible. Often, the individual sees him or herself very differently in a negative manner than he/she sees others. This individual can view someone who gives them attention as a superhuman being and miss the faults or idiosyncrasies of the other person. The individual who grew up with neglect can also either seek attention at any cost or can be stuck in his or her own belief that he/she is not worthy of anyone's attention.

Another challenge to discovering essence is understanding that we are living out of our reactions to our trauma. It takes faith and a belief that we are more than just a product of our environment. It also requires faith to believe that we have an identity that is healthy and is capable of living a happy, productive life that is also purpose motivated. When we live out of our essence we live according to our purpose and therefore, live a very happy life filled with contentment and peace. Personally, I believe this is impossible without having God in our life.

2

The Four Basic Points of Connection

Connection is what we are created for, many of us long for, and all of us are afraid of. Most of us are not aware of our fear of connection, but we definitely react out of our fear. I am convinced that most of our interactions with others have an element of fear. I also believe that all of our reactions to others are fear driven. Reactions are different than responses in that reactions are emotional and defensive.

Responses are calm, non-defensive, and seek understanding and positive connection. Therefore, any co Positive connections are non-defensive, matter of fact with nothing to prove, and seek knowledge and understanding of another human being. Negative connections are usually filled with defensiveness, an attempt to prove ourselves to others, and focused on ourselves showing no real interest in the other person. We choose on some level of consciousness what type of connection we want to have with the other person.

When we take a serious look at the way we interact with others and can honestly examine our side of those relationships; we have the ability to recognize our fears, our insecurities, and our ambivalence about relationships.

Ambivalence is a common reaction in relationships. The ambivalence is created due to our emotional need to protect ourselves from being hurt combined with our desire to be loved. Relationships trigger our trust issues. Relationships also trigger our insecurities. Are we good enough, are we lovable, does this person really care, will this person stay with me, is this person worthy of my heart are just some of the common questions we ask ourselves which helps to create ambivalence.

In addition to us feeling ambivalence, we also transmit ambivalence. We send out mixed messages. On one hand, we want to be able to receive love and give love freely and on the other hand, we are scared of being vulnerable, mistrust of receiving love, and fear of being rejected or even abandoned. It shows that we really do not know what we want and that we are very unsure of ourselves, especially when it comes to knowing what is best for us. I believe the more trauma that took place in our early life is directly related to the degree of our ambivalence.

When we are not aware of our past trauma, ambivalence can become more prevalent. Why? Because, we know that we are afraid, but we do not know why. It is like not knowing what you are searching for when you are already in a dark room. Our behaviors are driven by subconscious motives just as much as by conscious motives (Freud). And when our past is buried in our memory, our subconscious becomes stronger and thus our behaviors become more complex and perhaps strange, even to us. I discussed in the first chapter how trauma fragments the brain. Fragmentation can also manifest ambivalence.

Survivors of sexual abuse demonstrate significant ambivalence. Survivors of sexual abuse carry with them a heavy and complex façade. Often, survivors of sexual abuse are divided and not aware of being divided. Carolyn Braddock's work, Body Voices describes how survivors express their response to the trauma as well as their beliefs about themselves.

Carolyn Braddock discovered that feelings held deep within the body contribute to the development of certain body patterns. Braddock came up with three body types:

the rigid body, the collapsed body, and the inanimate body. The rigid body is where all the muscles and bones are stiff and the person moves in very defined, methodical motions and shows no fluidity. The collapsed body is where this person moves in very sloppy motions and it appears as if this person is attempting to hide. The inanimate body is where there is no gracefulness and there are no methodological movements. Braddock's work demonstrates that sexual trauma gets locked in the body as well as impacts the brain.

Another psychologist who believes that sexual trauma deeply affects the body is Peter Levine. Levine studied the imperative differences between how animals respond to trauma and how people respond to trauma. Levine's work in the area of biological psychology added to the field of neuroscience and trauma. In Levine's Somatic Experiencing therapy, Peter explains that with humans, trauma gets locked in the body, almost like a frozen state.

Peter goes onto explain that when animals are preyed upon, they rejuvenate almost immediately. This is not true for domesticated animals, like cats and dogs. However, animals living in the wild recoup as soon as their predator is gone. The human brain appears to lock traumatic incidents into our bodies and seems to store cognitive thought patterns and emotions about the event in the hippocampus part of our brains.

Several psychologists who have conducted research in this area and found very similar results include Bessel van der Kolk, Peter Levine, Carolyn Braddock, Nadine Burke Harris, Bruce Perry, and psychologists who work for the Kaiser Permanente, the CDC, and the Center for Youth Wellness are just a few of the many psychologists who have studied and concluded that early childhood trauma deeply affects the body and the brain. What I want the reader to understand are 1) there is a consensus that survivors of early trauma have been deeply impacted with severe negative consequences, including health problems later in life and 2) some of the negative consequences include poor communication and/or poor relationship skills, like knowing how to connect to another individual.

Survivors of early childhood trauma have learned how to connect to others in a very negative manner. While some survivors go on to become perpetrators; most survivors do not have any inkling to hurt another human being. The challenge is trust has been broken, safety has been ruined, and connection has been distorted.

In its place mistrust, defensiveness, and vigilance has been wired into the brain as normal ways to connect to others. This is why most psychologists and psychotherapists have agreed that in order to assist their clients in healing, safety, trust, and relationship must be the key components incorporated into therapy. Because we have been hurt in relationship, we must heal in relationship.

Healing is not an isolated event. I have had clients who have attempted to claim that a particular book has changed their life or has healed them. A particular book can enhance our thinking. No collection of books can change our emotions or can heal us. Life is meant to be lived on an experiential level, where we experience events, incidents (good and bad), and feel our emotions.

Living life on an emotional level is a significant component to living a self-actualized life. Communicating our emotions to another individual is the highest form of communication. When we share our emotions with one another is also the deepest level of intimacy. Any two individuals can share a sexual encounter with each other. Physical intimacy does not equate to emotional and spiritual intimacy.

In order to achieve emotional and spiritual intimacy, both individuals must first feel safe with each other. Then they must learn to trust each other over time. Thirdly, after safety and trust has been established in their relationship, then they must learn to speak each other's emotional language. After a series of consistent conversations involving sharing emotions, then emotional and spiritual connection is achieved.

The challenge is that many individuals are not aware of their lack of ability to connect to others. And, many individuals are not aware of all of their wounds or trauma which creates an inability to connect safely and confidently with others. As stated earlier, survivors of early childhood trauma often struggle with having generalized anxiety disorder, depression, social phobia, or other manifestations of mental and emotional malfunctioning. The other challenge is that often no one wants to spend time with someone who appears to be struggling emotionally or psychologically. So, the survivor's beliefs that he or she is not worthy or lovable becomes reinforced.

In spite that an individual may see him or herself as unworthy and unlovable, he or she may also have a closer connection to God than many others who have not had as much trauma or pain in their lives. Dr. Robert Grant, who wrote The Way of the Wound states his belief that behind the spirituality of some of the great spiritual leaders throughout the world are individual stories of significant trauma and deeply wounded individuals. Grant states, Trauma involves overwhelming life events that render most people powerless and/or living in fear for their life.

The major challenge of trauma is to integrate its impact into personal and collective frames of meaning. Trauma can shut down growth indefinitely on several, if not all, levels of one's being, depending on age, maturity, and type of trauma. These are just a few of the factors that influence the severity and intensity of the traumatic response. Differences in gender and age between the victim and perpetrator; the victim's relationship to the abuser, along with the availability of support, are other factors that influence the impact of trauma.

Unresolved trauma temporarily or permanently throws victims into a survival mode. Trauma disrupts abilities to form or maintain a self, along with abilities to develop increasingly more mature and flexible modes of relating. The traumatic response has a subjective component. Individuals exposed to the same traumatic event do not necessarily assign the same meaning. Meanings often depend upon ethnic, religious, familial and personal contributions, along with residues from previous trauma.

Trauma creates a false identity where an individual is behaving according to how an individual has interpreted his or her specific trauma and their perception of him or herself. Survivors of abuse become experts on creating stories or false beliefs of why they were abused. Beliefs such as I was born bad, I am a bad person and so bad things happen to me, or I'm stupid or deserving of bad events. Trauma often keeps individuals not only locked into a false identity, but also locked into a series of reactionary behaviors. Trauma separates us from our essence and replaces it with a false identity. God wants us to choose to heal and return us to our essence.

It is the most challenging journey we will ever decide to take in our lives. The journey is long and arduous. Psychologists who specialize in this area of trauma understands that the journey is arduous and long. As mentioned earlier, trauma affects the brain as well as the body. Levine explains it this way: One of the reasons why humans do not move in and out of the fight. flight, freeze response as naturally as animals is that humans have a highly evolved neo-cortex that is so complex and powerful that through fear and over control it can interfere with the subtle restorative instinctual impulses and responses.

Levine also explains how trauma affects the nervous system. The nervous system compensates for being in a state of self-perpetuating arousal by setting off a chain of adaptation that eventually bind and organize the energy into symptoms. The first symptoms of trauma usually appear shortly after the traumatic event that engendered them.

Other symptoms develop over time. Symptoms that develop last are excessive shyness, muted or diminished emotional responses, inability to make commitments, chronic fatigue, immune system problems such as thyroid dysfunction, psychosomatic illness, headaches, neck and back problems, asthma, digestive problems, severe premenstrual syndrome, depression, anxiety, feelings of impending doom, feelings of detachment, isolation, diminished interest in life, fear of dying, fear of going crazy, fear of shortened life, frequent crying, abrupt mood swings, rage reactions, temper tantrums, shame, diminished or exaggerated sexual activity, amnesia, forgetfulness, feelings, helplessness, inability to love, sleep disturbance, struggles with problem-solving skills, and challenges with dealing with stress. The inability to problem-solve and dealing with stress are challenges within the brain.

In addition to challenges and distress to the body and brain, survivors of early childhood trauma also endure challenges to the mind. I look at the brain as being in charge of processing information, communication, sorting through our emotions, and executing our behaviors. The mind is connected to the soul and is responsible for transferring messages to the brain. For example, it is our mind that receives and transfers messages such as I'm not lovable, I am a good person, No one can be trusted. These are not messages that were derived from logic. Rather, it is logic that must be used to sort through the message. Survivors of early childhood trauma usually have awful destructive messages from their mind, which adds to their low self-esteem.

So, we have discussed how trauma impacts the body, the brain, and our minds. Therefore, trauma impacts most aspects of our emotional lives. Trauma definitely impacts our emotional connections. When we are on the defense, don't know who we are, have difficulty trusting, and feeling very insecure connecting to others becomes a huge challenge. We all have listening filters. Our listening filters are based upon our perceptions and interpretations. Our perceptions and interpretations are formed from our experiences and previous knowledge. Therefore, the typical survivor is interpreting things that are said and done by others based upon our traumatic background. It becomes a challenge to view things without some type of projection.

Yet the one thing we are all looking for in relationship is to be heard and understood. We long to be in a relationship with someone who gets us. We fantasize about being someone who takes the time to listen to us, to understand us, and express empathy and compassion to us. The challenge is we must accept our projections, perceptions, and interpretations, in order to determine if we are listening and paying attention to the behaviors that actually reveal the authenticity of the person whom we are attempting to connect to. It requires two authentic individuals to have an authentic connection.

3

Understanding Attachment

It was the late 1930 s, when John Bowlby, a British psychiatrist, derived the theory of attachment. Bowlby's theory is that the relationship that we form with our primary caregiver during our early years (0 to 6) creates an internal working model (a mental imprinted blueprint) that acts as a template for all other relationships in our lives. This is the theory; nothing should be added and nothing should be deducted. Attachment is an extremely complex concept, a relatively new buzz word, something often overlooked and often misunderstood.

Over the past twenty years, much has been confused around the word attachment. I am going to be bold. In spite that many psychotherapists and psychologists discuss the concept of attachment in reference to the individuals whom we attach to; this is far from an accurate understanding of the concept of attachment. As stated in the previous paragraph, Bowlby made it very clear that attachment involves interacting with our internal working model. Therefore, in order to really understand attachment and in order to teach the true concept of attachment, it is imperative to understand what an internal working model is and what the role of an internal working model is.

My research on attachment has consistently shown that an internal working model can be defined as an internal mental blueprint for how we operate in the world. Research has also consistently shown that the purpose of our internal working model is to assimilate, as Piaget has shown us, new information into our preexisting schema.

It is our internal working model, our internal mental blueprint that guides our interactions, reactions, and responses to others and ourselves. For example, it is our internal working model that sorts out whether particular individuals can be trusted. It is also our internal working model that helps assist us in determining where to work, whether or not to pursue education, and what goals would be achievable for ourselves. As you can begin to understand our internal working model is the executive functioning device in our brains that is responsible for far more activity than whom we form relationships with.

This is why any individual who simply attempts to define attachment as the people whom we attach to is lacking a pure and true understanding of the concept of attachment. Attachment should not be viewed, defined, or assessed by the people whom we form relationship with alone. Attachment is the foundation for many aspects of our lives. Attachment is the internal infrastructure system one has inside (Bowlby s Internal Working Model) where all acts of confidence and motivation for our behavior comes from.

How is the internal infrastructure system created (Bowlby s Internal Working Model)? Attachment is an external process between the parent and the child that creates an intrinsic relationship. Attachment begins in utero at the time of conception. Babies in utero do feel the mother's stress, anxiety, and any ambivalence about the pregnancy. I often ask mothers about their pregnancy, and they often get the correlation between their child's anxiety and the anxiety the child felt in utero from the mother.

When the mother is taking good care of herself during pregnancy, she is also taking good care of her child. When the mother can live with little stress and anxiety, then the baby experiences little stress. When the birth is as natural and easy as possible, there is a greater chance of good attachment and low anxiety within the child. The next challenge to ease is bonding with the baby.

As I mentioned above, the manner in which the mother takes care of herself affects her baby in her womb. This is when and how emotional regulation begins. Emotional regulation is where mother learns that her baby's emotions are connected to her emotions. When mom is calm, baby is calm. When mom is angry or upset, baby is also upset.

When baby is upset but stays calm and holds and calms baby, the young child calms. Baby learns to copy mom's emotions. This process of mom calming her child and child copying mom's emotions continue throughout the child's early years (0-10), until the child begins to master how to calm themselves down. Then the child grows into a healthy adult who is able to 1) recognize what they are feeling, 2) be able to acknowledge what they are feeling and 3) be able to work through their emotions and achieve peace as a foundation and reach a place of emotional stability. Thus, emotional stability is a key component in attachment, a healthy internal working model, and positive mental wellness.

A significant component to emotional regulation is when the mother bonds with her baby. One of the most basic and common methods of bonding with your baby is breastfeeding.

There is a large body of research on the topics of how breastfeeding has been correlated with high intelligence in children. There is also a large body of research showing that breastfeeding is linked to a higher level of secure attachment in children. A vital part of the process of breastfeeding and attachment is the biological aspects.

The maximum distance that a baby can see is the exact distance between mom's eyes and her breast. In addition, there is the skin-to-skin contact that creates a bond between mom and her child, and this creates a relationship that is unique to the mother-child relationship. This is the foundation of the attachment process, where the infant is receiving most of her basic needs, which include food, warmth, being held, and comfort are greatly to the type of attachment (secure, fearful, dismissive, disorganized, preoccupied) her child will form.

The consistency of motherly behaviors toward her child has a lot to do with how a mother responds to her child's cries. Babies communicate through their cries. Babies cry for a reason. In past generations, parents were able to tell by the pitch of the baby's cry what the child was asking for. Due to parents having more insecure internal attachment patterns, parents have a much more difficult time in quickly recognizing their infant's needs. The sooner an infant has received his or her needs, the sooner that infant has been calmed and their stress has been eradicated. When our needs have been met, there is a stronger sense of gratification within us. We are happy when our needs are met and distressed when our needs are not met.

When our needs are met, we are happy because we feel safe and we feel safe because we can trust that we will be taken care of. We learn during our first year of life whether we can trust others. To an infant, their primary caregiver is seen as God, the person who is going to make everything okay, the person who will keep me safe, taken care of, and happy. As you know, the child's primary caregiver can be biological mom, biological dad, biological grandparent, adoptive parent, foster parent or another legal guardian.

Each individual has an internal working model (internal mental blueprint), a specific attachment pattern, whether it be secure, preoccupied, disorganized, fearful, or dismissive. It is the parent's internal attachment pattern that executes the parent's behaviors toward his or her child. A securely attached parent will most likely raise a child who will have secure attachment. However, it is far more difficult for a parent who has significantly insecure attachment patterns to raise a child with secure attachment. Our attachment patterns are hardwired and therefore become automatic responses to those around us that we are interacting with, including our children.

The good news is that in spite that our automatic responses to others, including our children are hardwired; we have the ability to learn new ways of relating to others. We can learn to become aware of our automatic responses as well as understand why we respond in the way that we do. When we become mindful of our actions and understand a new way of responding, we do have the power to raise our children better than how we were raised.

The key to doing anything better than our parents or doing anything better than what we have done is to be mindful of what we did and have the understanding to learn to do it different. It is true that fifty percent of everything we will learn in life from our birth to our death is learned during the first year of life. However, growth and knowledge are fluid. It is always up to us to determine how much we want to learn and how much we want to evolve toward living out of our essence.

In childhood, it is the parent that takes the lead in how the child will follow. When a parent is abusive toward a child, it is the child's interpretation of those abusive events that will contribute greatly to that child's success as well as the child's sense of value and the child's behaviors. When a parent is loving toward a child and has realistic observations of the child's abilities, the child will learn to be competent and achieve according to his or her full potential.

Abraham Maslow called this becoming self-actualized. The army calls it being all you can be. When a child is neglected, the child grows into an adult who does not value him/herself or relationships very much. Again, the ways in which we were raised, and our interpretations of those events becomes wired into our internal working model (our internal mental blueprint) and we react to the world according to our beliefs.

When our needs are met, we are happy and when our needs are not met, we become anxious, fearful, and mistrusting. Our internal working model is lacking a strong, dependable trustworthy internalized parent. The need to acquire an internalized parent who is trustworthy and is going to meet all of our needs and wants does not go away. It actually may intensify. Our need to have a strong reliable trustworthy internalized parent gets played out in our romantic relationships.

As a couples' coach and marriage and family counselor, I have found that at the very root of the majority of issues in a romantic relationship lies two wounded and hurting children in adult bodies. Each individual in the relationship is looking to the other to become his or her safe, trustworthy, reliable internalized parent who will make the other person happy. I also believe that when this internalized parent shows a lack of reliability or unworthiness, that the individual feels hurt and reacts with anger. That anger could be manifested in cheating on their lover, withdrawing, or behaving in passive-aggressive manners.

A good relationship counselor is needed at this point in order to prevent further destructiveness in the relationship. The couple should be seeking a professional who truly understands attachment and psychodynamic paradigms in order to assist the couple in understanding how their childhoods have gotten entangled. It is also a painful lesson to learn that we adults cannot find our internalized parent in another adult. And, when we subconsciously or consciously attempt to acquire our internalized parent in a romantic relationship, we end up creating an entangled web of unmet emotional needs. A healthy relationship requires two healthy adults.

Different psychologists over time have derived their own definition of a healthy adult. Erickson created eight stages of psychosocial development with the first stage of trust versus mistrust occurring during infancy. Erickson and Freud clearly stated that it is necessary to achieve each stage of development successfully in order to achieve a mentally healthy adulthood. Erickson also stated that the most significant stage of development is trust versus mistrust. John Bowlby, the father of attachment also stated that trust is the core element in healthy relationships. Bowlby also created the first year and second year bonding cycles explain how trust or mistrust is created.

Using Bowlby's internal working model, we can begin to evaluate our adult relationships along with our mental wellness. Start with the basic question: How much do you trust your lover, friends, others, etc.? This is also an evaluative tool to determine where in our development lies our wounds. Trust is the foundation of all our relationships, including the one we have or don't have with God.

As we continue to build on our development, we move from trust onto learning boundaries. In the second and third years of life, attachment becomes strengthened through the parent teaching the child limits and boundaries in a healthy and safe environment. Children must learn at a young age (2 to 6) that safety and protection involve boundaries. You don't drive at whatever speed feels good to you. If you put your hand on a hot stove, you will get burned. There are limitations to how much one can eat before getting sick.

Limitations and boundaries are for our benefit to keep us safe and healthy. When we have learned to trust, it becomes much easier to understand that limitations and boundaries are for our benefit. It is during these first three years of life, where our self-esteem is being enhanced, where we learn to face challenges and to learn that attempting the challenge like learning something new is more important than the result or outcome. This is a vital component for the foundation of attachment.

Another significant component for the foundation of attachment is the infrastructure system attachment creates. As stated earlier, Bowlby called this infrastructure system the internal working model. Starting at an early age, we thrive when we have structure, and we struggle when we don't have structure. So, let's define structure.

Structure involves consistency, dependability, and predictability. A consistent set of rules, consequences, expectations, routines, rituals, and responsibilities helps significantly to create structure. Other aspects of creating structure involve the emotional stability of the individual who is attempting to maintain structure. Remember Bowlby's second year bonding cycle where trust, bonding, and deeper attachment are formed, when structure, including setting limits and boundaries are done on a consistent basis.

People function at a much higher level and demonstrate more happiness when they know what they are supposed to be doing and why. I believe this is one of the reasons why individuals usually prefer to attend school over work. When you are in school you know that you need to study in order to learn particular material and to pass an exam. An assignment might seem dumb to you. However, you also assign purpose to completing that dumb assignment by understanding that the completion of the assignment is necessary in order to acquire a good grade. One of the things that I miss about college is preparing for the next semester.

I found it very interesting to read about what I would be learning in the next several weeks and it was for a purpose. When an intelligent individual finds that the only purpose to working at a job that is not very fulfilling is to earn money to survive; there is stronger likelihood for depression and an unsatisfied life. So, a significant part of structure must involve purpose, in order to achieve what Maslow called being self-actualized.

The lower needs of Maslow's Hierarchy involve shelter, food, and safety. All of which should be consistent and should be the foundation of anyone's life. When we eat at the same time, go to bed at the same time, and awake at the same time, we have created a healthy consistent structure. The manifestations of structure are higher self-esteem, security, a healthy understanding of boundaries, a healthy understanding of appropriate behavior according to the time and place.

In addition, structure creates a healthy built-in safety net that tells us that when one thing doesn't work out, there will be opportunity for something else. When one door closes, perhaps a window will open. A built-in safety net is also necessary to be okay with risk. Life is filled with risks, however the number one reason why individuals are not willing to risk is that they do not feel that they will be okay if they were to fail. Structure also creates a built-in template for problem-solving. Structure creates a healthy internal infrastructure system, which creates healthy self-esteem.

Healthy self-esteem is not having everything easy or handed to us. Everyone on a team receiving a trophy does not create true healthy self-esteem. Rather, healthy self-esteem is having the ability and willingness to accept what they are good at and accepting what they are not good at and being okay with that. Healthy self-esteem is recognizing that there are particular areas that we have to work harder at than everyone else. Healthy self-esteem actually helps us become truly humble because we recognize people are not created with equal talent, knowledge, or intelligence. There will be areas that others will exceed well beyond your abilities and there are probably things that you will exceed at beyond other individuals.

One of the huge complexities if achieving true self-esteem is understanding our uniqueness. Perhaps, one of the greatest gifts we can give to another human being is truly seeing him or her as he or she actually is. Being able to stop projecting and stop expecting someone to be who he or she is not can be a great challenge for most of us. We want people to be who we want them to be and to act in ways that are pleasing to us. It is difficult for us to truly comprehend that others don't often share our viewpoints. This becomes very obvious when individuals argue politics. It is the rare individual who wants to be educated by someone else's views.

It is our experiences in life that help form our views. Our views express a significant part of our identity. Our views comprise of our cultural background, our education, our values, our childhood influences, and our experiences. It is how we integrate our views and beliefs into our daily lives that express our intelligence, our creativity, and our passions in life. There are people who are very passionate about politics and play a role in who gets elected. There are some people who want to make a positive change through teaching, preaching, working as a doctor, nurse, or attorney. There are other individuals who work for a positive change one person at a time, like a psychologist or mentor. And there are other individuals who want to work for a positive change through architecture, engineering, or working to make positive changes to our environment, which obviously affects all of us.

One of our challenges is that only a few individuals in the world achieve the opportunity to discover their passions and to work for positive changes in our communities or the world. We all have a very basic need to survive. If we are focused on just surviving, there is little resources, including time, money, and energy to work toward positive changes for others, let alone society. We need more resources for more individuals to achieve discovering their essence.

When individuals live out of their essence, there is more likelihood of achievement in scholarly attributes. Essence does not guarantee a college degree or a successful business career. What essence does guarantee is contentment. Living out of essence also guarantees that we will achieve our highest level of potential. If an individual has a low IQ and is limited in his or her own resources, but is living in his or her essence, that individual will be successful because he/she has accomplished his or her highest level of achievement. Western society often assigns success with finances and status. Not every wealthy individual is successful and not every poor person is a failure.

When a person is living out of his or her essence, it means that he or she has achieved success. Success should be based upon how much an individual has reached his or her fullest potential and purpose in life.

When we are living out of our essence, we have reached self-actualization, the highest level on Maslow's hierarchy of needs. Individuals who have accomplished this have no desire nor need to compare themselves to others. This individual is content, happy, and has found and accomplished his or her purpose in life. I believe many of our forefathers lived out of their essence. I believe the saints in the Christian church, like Mother Teresa, Apostle Paul, Peter, and John achieved this level of humanity.

So, how did these individuals achieve this level of humanity? I won't be dissecting their journeys in this book. I just want to point out that it is a possible goal. And I believe that one of the common traits of these individuals is that each of these individuals used his or her past to discover their purpose and while discovering their purpose they discovered their essence.

The purpose of this book is to help the reader learn the journey of discovering your essence. I also believe that whether you search for your essence or you search for your purpose in this life, you will find both about the same time. This is because they are connected.

We have been discussing attachment during this chapter. I stated earlier that the easiest way to determine if someone truly understands attachment is listening for that individual to discuss how attachment is internal and to listen for that individual to discuss the internal working model of an individual.

I also began to discuss how our attachment process goes awry is through experiencing trauma in our early lives during the attachment process. A significant component of the attachment process is the beliefs that parents or caregivers give to children. For example, an abusive parent often gives the message to his or her child that the child is not worth much and is deserving of being treated badly. Another example is the narcissistic parent who often gives the message to his or her child that the child could do no wrong and that the child is more special than everyone else.

In both cases, the child is growing up with false beliefs about him/herself. These false beliefs are a vital part of having a buried essence. Neil Anderson says we have no other choice but to behave according to what we believe. We learn this through interviews, sometimes painfully. We can think one thing about ourselves and find out that others do not see it the same way. Individuals who have grown up with abuse in their childhood, usually don't have very high expectations of themselves. And, this same individual who struggles with low self-esteem usually conveys his or her low self-esteem in their communication, how they dress, how they present themselves and sometimes even in their walk. The way in which we were treated by the people whom we were supposed to trust the most has formed a template for us to interpret all new information.

This is John Bowlby's attachment theory. Bowlby called this internal template the internal working model. The attachment process is biological, sensory integrative, emotional, cognitive, and behavioral. It is the process that involves all of the parent-child activities that take place during the child's first six years of life. The cognitive and emotional aspects of the parent-child relationship involve the messages that the child is receiving and interpreting.

When a parent conveys love to his or child through attentiveness, interest, extending care and positive emotions and attitude toward the child, the child interprets these messages as love and that the child can trust the parent. When trust and safety are interpreted by the child, the child becomes an individual who is more likely to listen to his or her parents and be compliant. You can often tell that a child is loved by his or her parents without even knowing the parents. For example, how a young child behaves in childcare or school demonstrates that he or she is loved at home.

How? When safety and trust become wired/integrated into a child's internal working model, the child becomes obedient. Why? Because the child is not questioning the rules set by adults, rather the child is expecting that the adult caregiver is telling the child something to do which is in the child's best interest.

Trust follows safety and being cared for. And obedience follows trust. This does not mean that the child will always obey and always listen and follow directions. Children also have free-will and want to rebel at any age in an attempt to explore their environment. The mentally well parent also understands that they are not perfect, and they can accept that they will make mistakes and their child will at times disobey.

The mentally healthy parent sees their child objectively. This means that the parent can separate their child's behavior from the identity of the child. It means that the parent can understand that his or her child can be acting out or disobeying out of rebelliousness, frustration, anger, or grief and sadness. The mentally well parent sees his or her child for the person whom God created that child to become. Many parents, unfortunately, want to see their child as a star athlete, in spite that the child has limited talent in being an athlete. Other parents want to live vicariously through their child and attempt to project (make their child out to be whom the parent wanted to be).

The mentally well parent recognizes who the child is, what talents the child actually has and what talents the child does not have. The mentally healthy parent maintains the attachment with his or her child through recognizing who the child is and recognizes what the child is capable of , what the child is not capable of and that their child has a full range of emotions and will probably disobey and dislike the parent at times.

Children often test their parents to determine whether they are still loved. In addition, children will often test the boundaries set by their parents to determine if they are still safe and trustworthy parents. Trust is earned over time through consistent acts of getting our needs met. Children instinctively understand this and actually form their own evaluations of whether they have a trustworthy parent. This process of determining if we can trust whether we will be taken care of and have our needs met is what I call the cognitive component of the attachment process.

The next component of attachment is the emotional component. I believe the emotional component is most closely related to the cognitive component. In the previous paragraph, we discussed the cognitive component, where even babies and young children evaluate the degree of trust they can have with their caregivers. The emotional component deals with the same process of trust being equated with needs being met. I am only separating them out here to express to the reader that babies communicate by crying. God has wired emotions into each of our brains.

Expressing emotions is the deepest level of intimacy between two individuals. In order to feel comfortable to express our emotions, three elements must be present. First, we must be willing to face our insecurities, second, we must feel that the other person is safe for us to express our emotions, and third, we must trust the other person in order to expose ourselves emotionally.

Our early evaluations of trust and safety based upon our cognitive and emotional processes during the early attachment process becomes wired in our brains at an early age. This is what Bowlby called the Internal Working Model.

Remember, Bowlby stated that our internal working model is the template that is formed during our attachment process that demonstrates that all intimate relationships in our lives are based upon the early relationship we formed with our primary caregiver during our early years of life.

We react and interact in our adult relationships in the manner that got programmed into our young brains while interacting with our primary caregiver. We often feel similar emotions. If our early relationship created anxiety, then we feel anxiety in our adult relationships. On the other hand, if our parents were able to form a strong, secure attachment with us when we were young, then we will feel confident and secure in connecting with another individual as an adult.

Our sense of security lies inside of our internal working model. The attachment process is intense, and it is a vital part of our identity as well as an imperative part of our behavior. Our identity begins to form in the womb. Attachment begins with conception. Another significant component of the attachment process is the biological component. During the period of pregnancy, the mother is the major provider for her child through taking care of her own physical needs and maintaining good health that the mother is delivering a message of love to her child. The child also receives the message of whether he/she is a wanted baby.

The birth process is supposed to be intentionally set up for the child to be welcomed into the world. Just as much as the child is receiving love, the welcoming and acceptance of the child brings love to the parents. At least, this is what is supposed to happen. The ideal connection between two human beings is the reciprocity of love, giving and receiving of love. The mother providing milk to her infant child through her breast creates a positive attachment that also creates safety and trust. The mother and child are becoming a unit. The mother and infant are creating a symbiotic relationship. The mother is becoming imprinted into the child's DNA.

Bruce Perry once said that the child's DNA is correlated with the child's environment and that the child's environment dictates the child's DNA. This begins with the birth process. This is the root of the biological makeup of a child. An infant receives his/her oxygen and nutrients through the umbilical cord. In addition, the umbilical cord is basically a lifeline between the mother and infant.

It is through this lifeline (umbilical cord) that the infant also receives messages that life is good or life is a struggle. This is the first time that Bowlby's bonding cycle, where trust is formed when basic needs are met. Unfortunately, it is also the foundation where attachment and trust can go awry. When pregnant mothers use alcohol or drugs, the alcohol and drugs get transmitted to the infant through the umbilical cord and usually causes significant damage to the infant's brain. The cry of a baby who is healthy is very different than the cry of an addicted baby or a baby who has been traumatized. The biological process can go positive or negative extremely similar to the cognitive and emotional processes of attachment.

When the biological process goes positive, along with the emotional and cognitive processes of attachment, then safety and trust are formed, and security is wired inside the child's internal working model. When the biological process goes awry, then the emotional and cognitive processes of attachment will most likely also go awry creating a lack of trust, a lack of safety and insecurity to be wired inside the child's internal working model.

As I incorporated the biological, cognitive, and emotional components of the attachment process, all of the components of attachment work together to create the internal working model. The only reason why I separated the individual components of attachment is to demonstrate to the reader the understanding of how each component has its individual purpose, responsibility, and actions. However, it is the integration of all of the components that comprise the attachment process.

In addition to the biological, cognitive, and emotional components is the behavioral component of the attachment process. Here are some questions that can help to determine the assessment of attachment: Did the mother demonstrate during pregnancy that her child will be welcomed into the world? Was the child shown loving acts of trust and safety toward the child? Is the child being taken care of? Does each parent demonstrate a loving positive attitude toward the child? Does each parent spend significant time holding the child? Does the parent give the baby massages and gentle, loving touch? Does the parent play with the child? These last three questions demonstrate the behavioral component of the attachment process.

Since love is demonstrative and we were wired by God for positive touch, it would make sense that touch or the parent's behavior toward the child is a significant component of the attachment process. The parent's behavior toward the child is another component that could be either positive or negative. Remember, it is consistency not constancy that is the possibility and the goal.

Does the parent's behavior toward the child show a consistent pattern of positive interaction or a negative interaction with the child? A significant part of my dissertation studied how the parent's attitude plays a significant role in the success of that child. Children figure out their environment by collecting all the data from their parents, process it in their own ways, interpret the data and then often play out their interpretations of that data. Children are sponges to their environment. They soak in the data, interpret it and then often replicate their interpretations through their behavior.

A person's behavior reveals that individual's beliefs. A person's beliefs are often formed or created early on in life through our interpretations of significant events and often by the behaviors and attitudes of significant people in our lives. Children will not remember everything. However, children will always remember how important they are to the people whom were most important to them.

Children learn through their five senses, and they form their interpretations from the input of the data through their senses. So, another component of the attachment process is the sensory integration component. This refers to the five senses and how learning, especially for a child takes place through the integration of all of our senses.

All this information, this culmination of data collected from conception through the early years of life (age 6), is inputted into the brain almost like a computer program and the child's internal working model is created

Hopefully, you are putting the puzzle together that the child's internal working model is the executive director for the child's beliefs and behaviors. This is why I believe that attachment is at the core foundation for most psychological pathology.

When we have secure attachment, we have a strong positive internal working model with a high sense of security, which connects us to our essence. When we have a form of insecure attachment, we have a weak and struggling internal working model with a high sense of insecurity, which connects us to a false identity. Over the past twenty years, much has been confused around the word attachment.

I am going to be bold. In spite that many psychotherapists and psychologists discuss the concept of attachment in reference to the individuals whom we attach to; this is far from an accurate understanding of the concept of attachment. As stated in the previous paragraph, Bowlby made it very clear that attachment involves interacting with our internal working model. Therefore, in order to really understand attachment and in order to teach the true concept of attachment, it is imperative to understand what an internal working model is and what the role of an internal working model is.

My research on attachment has consistently shown that an internal working model can be defined as an internal mental blueprint for how we operate in the world. Research has also consistently shown that the purpose of our internal working model is to assimilate, as Piaget has shown us, new information into our preexisting schema.

It is our internal working model, our internal mental blueprint that guides our interactions, reactions, and responses to others and ourselves. For example, it is our internal working model that sorts out whether particular individuals can be trusted. It is also our internal working model that helps assist us in determining where to work, whether or not to pursue education, and what goals would be achievable for ourselves. As you can begin to understand our internal working model is the executive functioning device in our brains that is responsible for far more activity than whom we form relationships with.

This is why any individual who simply attempts to define attachment as the people whom we attach to is lacking a pure and true understanding of the concept of attachment. Attachment should not be viewed, defined, or assessed by the people whom we form relationship with alone. Attachment is the foundation for many aspects of our lives. Attachment is the internal infrastructure system one has inside (Bowlby s Internal Working Model) where all acts of confidence and motivation for our behavior comes from.

How is the internal infrastructure system created (Bowlby s Internal Working Model)? Attachment is an external process between the parent and the child that creates an intrinsic relationship. Attachment begins in utero at the time of conception. Babies in utero do feel the mother's stress, anxiety, and any ambivalence about the pregnancy. I often ask mothers about their pregnancy, and they often get the correlation between their child's anxiety and the anxiety the child felt in utero from the mother.

When the mother is taking good care of herself during pregnancy, she is also taking good care of her child. When the mother can live with little stress and anxiety, then the baby experiences little stress. When the birth is as natural and easy as possible, there is a greater chance of good attachment and low anxiety within the child. The next challenge to ease is bonding with the baby.

As I mentioned above, the manner in which the mother takes care of herself affects her baby in her womb. This is when and how emotional regulation begins. Emotional regulation is where mother learns that her baby's emotions are connected to her emotions. When mom is calm, baby is calm. When mom is angry or upset, baby is also upset.

When baby is upset but stays calm and holds and calms baby, the young child calms. Baby learns to copy mom's emotions. This process of mom calming her child and child copying mom's emotions continue throughout the child's early years (0-10), until the child begins to master how to calm themselves down.

Then the child grows into a healthy adult who is able to 1) recognize what they are feeling, 2) be able to acknowledge what they are feeling and 3) be able to work through their emotions and achieve peace as a foundation and reach a place of emotional stability. Thus, emotional stability is a key component in attachment, a healthy internal working model, and positive mental wellness.

A significant component to emotional regulation is when the mother bonds with her baby. One of the most basic and common methods of bonding with your baby is breastfeeding.

There is a large body of research on the topics of how breastfeeding has been correlated with high intelligence in children. There is also a large body of research showing that breastfeeding is linked to a higher level of secure attachment in children. A vital part of the process of breastfeeding and attachment is the biological aspects.

The maximum distance that a baby can see is the exact distance between mom's eyes and her breast. In addition, there is the skin-to-skin contact that creates a bond between mom and her child, and this creates a relationship that is unique to the mother-child relationship. This is the foundation of the attachment process, where the infant is receiving most of her basic needs, which include food, warmth, being held, and comfort are greatly to the type of attachment (secure, fearful, dismissive, disorganized, preoccupied) her child will form.

The consistency of motherly behaviors toward her child has a lot to do with how a mother responds to her child's cries. Babies communicate through their cries. Babies cry for a reason. In past generations, parents were able to tell by the pitch of the baby's cry what the child was asking for. Due to parents having more insecure internal attachment patterns, parents have a much more difficult time in quickly recognizing their infant's needs.

The sooner an infant has received his or her needs, the sooner that infant has been calmed and their stress has been eradicated. When our needs have been met, there is a stronger sense of gratification within us. We are happy when our needs are met and distressed when our needs are not met.

When our needs are met, we are happy because we feel safe and we feel safe because we can trust that we will be taken care of. We learn during our first year of life whether we can trust others. To an infant, their primary caregiver is seen as God, the person who is going to make everything okay, the person who will keep me safe, taken care of, and happy. As you know, the child's primary caregiver can be biological mom, biological dad, biological grandparent, adoptive parent, foster parent or another legal guardian.

Each individual has an internal working model (internal mental blueprint), a specific attachment pattern, whether it be secure, preoccupied, disorganized, fearful, or dismissive. It is the parent's internal attachment pattern that executes the parent's behaviors toward his or her child. A securely attached parent will most likely raise a child who will have secure attachment. However, it is far more difficult for a parent who has significantly insecure attachment patterns to raise a child with secure attachment. Our attachment patterns are hardwired and therefore become automatic responses to those around us that we are interacting with, including our children.

The good news is that in spite that our automatic responses to others, including our children are hardwired; we have the ability to learn new ways of relating to others. We can learn to become aware of our automatic responses as well as understand why we respond in the way that we do. When we become mindful of our actions and understand a new way of responding, we do have the power to raise our children better than how we were raised.

The key to doing anything better than our parents or doing anything better than what we have done is to be mindful of what we did and have the understanding to learn to do it different. It is true that fifty percent of everything we will learn in life from our birth to our death is learned during the first year of life. However, growth and knowledge are fluid. It is always up to us to determine how much we want to learn and how much we want to evolve toward living out of our essence.

In childhood, it is the parent that takes the lead in how the child will follow. When a parent is abusive toward a child, it is the child's interpretation of those abusive events that will contribute greatly to that child's success as well as the child's sense of value and the child's behaviors. When a parent is loving toward a child and has realistic observations of the child's abilities, the child will learn to be competent and achieve according to his or her full potential.

Abraham Maslow called this becoming self-actualized. The army calls it being all you can be. When a child is neglected, the child grows into an adult who does not value him/herself or relationships very much. Again, the ways in which we were raised, and our interpretations of those events becomes wired into our internal working model (our internal mental blueprint) and we react to the world according to our beliefs.

When our needs are met, we are happy and when our needs are not met, we become anxious, fearful, and mistrusting. Our internal working model is lacking a strong, dependable trustworthy internalized parent. The need to acquire an internalized parent who is trustworthy and is going to meet all of our needs and wants does not go away. It actually may intensify. Our need to have a strong reliable trustworthy internalized parent gets played out in our romantic relationships.

As a couples' coach and marriage and family counselor, I have found that at the very root of the majority of issues in a romantic relationship lies two wounded and hurting children in adult bodies. Each individual in the relationship is looking to the other to become his or her safe, trustworthy, reliable internalized parent who will make the other person happy. I also believe that when this internalized parent shows a lack of reliability or unworthiness, that the individual feels hurt and reacts with anger. That anger could be manifested in cheating on their lover, withdrawing, or behaving in passive-aggressive manners.

A good relationship counselor is needed at this point in order to prevent further destructiveness in the relationship. The couple should be seeking a professional who truly understands attachment and psychodynamic paradigms in order to assist the couple in understanding how their childhoods have gotten entangled. It is also a painful lesson to learn that we adults cannot find our internalized parent in another adult. And, when we subconsciously or consciously attempt to acquire our internalized parent in a romantic relationship, we end up creating an entangled web of unmet emotional needs. A healthy relationship requires two healthy adults.

Different psychologists over time have derived their own definition of a healthy adult. Erickson created eight stages of psychosocial development with the first stage of trust versus mistrust occurring during infancy. Erickson and Freud clearly stated that it is necessary to achieve each stage of development successfully in order to achieve a mentally healthy adulthood. Erickson also stated that the most significant stage of development is trust versus mistrust. John Bowlby, the father of attachment also stated that trust is the core element in healthy relationships. Bowlby also created the first year and second year bonding cycles explain how trust or mistrust is created.

Using Bowlby's internal working model, we can begin to evaluate our adult relationships along with our mental wellness. Start with the basic question: How much do you trust your lover, friends, others, etc.? This is also an evaluative tool to determine where in our development lies our wounds. Trust is the foundation of all our relationships, including the one we have or don't have with God.

As we continue to build on our development, we move from trust onto learning boundaries. In the second and third years of life, attachment becomes strengthened through the parent teaching the child limits and boundaries in a healthy and safe environment. Children must learn at a young age (2 to 6) that safety and protection involve boundaries. You don't drive at whatever speed feels good to you. If you put your hand on a hot stove, you will get burned. There are limitations to how much one can eat before getting sick.

Limitations and boundaries are for our benefit to keep us safe and healthy. When we have learned to trust, it becomes much easier to understand that limitations and boundaries are for our benefit. It is during these first three years of life, where our self-esteem is being enhanced, where we learn to face challenges and to learn that attempting the challenge like learning something new is more important than the result or outcome. This is a vital component for the foundation of attachment.

Another significant component for the foundation of attachment is the infrastructure system attachment creates. As stated earlier, Bowlby called this infrastructure system the internal working model. Starting at an early age, we thrive when we have structure, and we struggle when we don't have structure. So, let's define structure.

Structure involves consistency, dependability, and predictability. A consistent set of rules, consequences, expectations, routines, rituals, and responsibilities helps significantly to create structure. Other aspects of creating structure involve the emotional stability of the individual who is attempting to maintain structure. Remember Bowlby's second year bonding cycle where trust, bonding, and deeper attachment are formed, when structure, including setting limits and boundaries are done on a consistent basis.

People function at a much higher level and demonstrate more happiness when they know what they are supposed to be doing and why. I believe this is one of the reasons why individuals usually prefer to attend school over work. When you are in school you know that you need to study in order to learn particular material and to pass an exam. An assignment might seem dumb to you. However, you also assign purpose to completing that dumb assignment by understanding that the completion of the assignment is necessary in order to acquire a good grade. One of the things that I miss about college is preparing for the next semester.

I found it very interesting to read about what I would be learning in the next several weeks and it was for a purpose. When an intelligent individual finds that the only purpose to working at a job that is not very fulfilling is to earn money to survive; there is stronger likelihood for depression and an unsatisfied life. So, a significant part of structure must involve purpose, in order to achieve what Maslow called being self-actualized.

The lower needs of Maslow's Hierarchy involve shelter, food, and safety. All of which should be consistent and should be the foundation of anyone's life. When we eat at the same time, go to bed at the same time, and awake at the same time, we have created a healthy consistent structure. The manifestations of structure are higher self-esteem, security, a healthy understanding of boundaries, a healthy understanding of appropriate behavior according to the time and place.

In addition, structure creates a healthy built-in safety net that tells us that when one thing doesn't work out, there will be opportunity for something else. When one door closes, perhaps a window will open. A built-in safety net is also necessary to be okay with risk. Life is filled with risks, however the number one reason why individuals are not willing to risk is that they do not feel that they will be okay if they were to fail. Structure also creates a built-in template for problem-solving. Structure creates a healthy internal infrastructure system, which creates healthy self-esteem.

Healthy self-esteem is not having everything easy or handed to us. Everyone on a team receiving a trophy does not create true healthy self-esteem. Rather, healthy self-esteem is having the ability and willingness to accept what they are good at and accepting what they are not good at and being okay with that. Healthy self-esteem is recognizing that there are particular areas that we have to work harder at than everyone else. Healthy self-esteem actually helps us become truly humble because we recognize people are not created with equal talent, knowledge, or intelligence. There will be areas that others will exceed well beyond your abilities and there are probably things that you will exceed at beyond other individuals.

One of the huge complexities if achieving true self-esteem is understanding our uniqueness. Perhaps, one of the greatest gifts we can give to another human being is truly seeing him or her as he or she actually is. Being able to stop projecting and stop expecting someone to be who he or she is not can be a great challenge for most of us. We want people to be who we want them to be and to act in ways that are pleasing to us. It is difficult for us to truly comprehend that others don't often share our viewpoints. This becomes very obvious when individuals argue politics. It is the rare individual who wants to be educated by someone else's views.

It is our experiences in life that help form our views. Our views express a significant part of our identity. Our views comprise of our cultural background, our education, our values, our childhood influences, and our experiences.

It is how we integrate our views and beliefs into our daily lives that express our intelligence, our creativity, and our passions in life.

There are people who are very passionate about politics and play a role in who gets elected. There are some people who want to make a positive change through teaching, preaching, working as a doctor, nurse, or attorney. There are other individuals who work for a positive change one person at a time, like a psychologist or mentor. And there are other individuals who want to work for a positive change through architecture, engineering, or working to make positive changes to our environment, which obviously affects all of us.

One of our challenges is that only a few individuals in the world achieve the opportunity to discover their passions and to work for positive changes in our communities or the world. We all have a very basic need to survive. If we are focused on just surviving, there is little resources, including time, money, and energy to work toward positive changes for others, let alone society. We need more resources for more individuals to achieve discovering their essence.

When individuals live out of their essence, there is more likelihood of achievement in scholarly attributes. Essence does not guarantee a college degree or a successful business career. What essence does guarantee is contentment. Living out of essence also guarantees that we will achieve our highest level of potential.

If an individual has a low IQ and is limited in his or her own resources, but is living in his or her essence, that individual will be successful because he/she has accomplished his or her highest level of achievement. Western society often assigns success with finances and status. Not every wealthy individual is successful and not every poor person is a failure.

When a person is living out of his or her essence, it means that he or she has achieved success. Success should be based upon how much an individual has reached his or her fullest potential and purpose in life.

When we are living out of our essence, we have reached self-actualization, the highest level on Maslow's hierarchy of needs. Individuals who have accomplished this have no desire nor need to compare themselves to others. This individual is content, happy, and has found and accomplished his or her purpose in life. I believe many of our forefathers lived out of their essence. I believe the saints in the Christian church, like Mother Teresa, Apostle Paul, Peter, and John achieved this level of humanity.

So, how did these individuals achieve this level of humanity? I won't be dissecting their journeys in this book. I just want to point out that it is a possible goal. And I believe that one of the common traits of these individuals is that each of these individuals used his or her past to discover their purpose and while discovering their purpose they discovered their essence.

The purpose of this book is to help the reader learn the journey of discovering your essence. I also believe that whether you search for your essence or you search for your purpose in this life, you will find both about the same time. This is because they are connected.

We have been discussing attachment during this chapter. I stated earlier that the easiest way to determine if someone truly understands attachment is listening for that individual to discuss how attachment is internal and to listen for that individual to discuss the internal working model of an individual.

I also began to discuss how our attachment process goes awry is through experiencing trauma in our early lives during the attachment process. A significant component of the attachment process is the beliefs that parents or caregivers give to children. For example, an abusive parent often gives the message to his or her child that the child is not worth much and is deserving of being treated badly. Another example is the narcissistic parent who often gives the message to his or her child that the child could do no wrong and that the child is more special than everyone else.

In both cases, the child is growing up with false beliefs about him/herself. These false beliefs are a vital part of having a buried essence. Neil Anderson says we have no other choice but to behave according to what we believe.

We learn this through interviews, sometimes painfully. We can think one thing about ourselves and find out that others do not see it the same way. Individuals who have grown up with abuse in their childhood, usually don't have very high expectations of themselves. And, this same individual who struggles with low self-esteem usually conveys his or her low self-esteem in their communication, how they dress, how they present themselves and sometimes even in their walk. The way in which we were treated by the people whom we were supposed to trust the most has formed a template for us to interpret all new information.

This is John Bowlby's attachment theory. Bowlby called this internal template the internal working model. The attachment process is biological, sensory integrative, emotional, cognitive, and behavioral. It is the process that involves all of the parent-child activities that take place during the child's first six years of life. The cognitive and emotional aspects of the parent-child relationship involve the messages that the child is receiving and interpreting.

When a parent conveys love to his or child through attentiveness, interest, extending care and positive emotions and attitude toward the child, the child interprets these messages as love and that the child can trust the parent. When trust and safety are interpreted by the child, the child becomes an individual who is more likely to listen to his or her parents and be compliant. You can often tell that a child is loved by his or her parents without even knowing the parents. For example, how a young child behaves in childcare or school demonstrates that he or she is loved at home.

How? When safety and trust become wired/integrated into a child's internal working model, the child becomes obedient. Why? Because the child is not questioning the rules set by adults, rather the child is expecting that the adult caregiver is telling the child something to do which is in the child's best interest.

Trust follows safety and being cared for. And obedience follows trust. This does not mean that the child will always obey and always listen and follow directions. Children also have free-will and want to rebel at any age in an attempt to explore their environment. The mentally well parent also understands that they are not perfect, and they can accept that they will make mistakes and their child will at times disobey.

The mentally healthy parent sees their child objectively. This means that the parent can separate their child's behavior from the identity of the child. It means that the parent can understand that his or her child can be acting out or disobeying out of rebelliousness, frustration, anger, or grief and sadness. The mentally well parent sees his or her child for the person whom God created that child to become. Many parents, unfortunately, want to see their child as a star athlete, in spite that the child has limited talent in being an athlete. Other parents want to live vicariously through their child and attempt to project (make their child out to be whom the parent wanted to be).

The mentally well parent recognizes who the child is, what talents the child actually has and what talents the child does not have. The mentally healthy parent maintains the attachment with his or her child through recognizing who the child is and recognizes what the child is capable of , what the child is not capable of and that their child has a full range of emotions and will probably disobey and dislike the parent at times.

Children often test their parents to determine whether they are still loved. In addition, children will often test the boundaries set by their parents to determine if they are still safe and trustworthy parents. Trust is earned over time through consistent acts of getting our needs met. Children instinctively understand this and actually form their own evaluations of whether they have a trustworthy parent. This process of determining if we can trust whether we will be taken care of and have our needs met is what I call the cognitive component of the attachment process.

The next component of attachment is the emotional component. I believe the emotional component is most closely related to the cognitive component. In the previous paragraph, we discussed the cognitive component, where even babies and young children evaluate the degree of trust they can have with their caregivers. The emotional component deals with the same process of trust being equated with needs being met. I am only separating them out here to express to the reader that babies communicate by crying. God has wired emotions into each of our brains.

Expressing emotions is the deepest level of intimacy between two individuals. In order to feel comfortable to express our emotions, three elements must be present. First, we must be willing to face our insecurities, second, we must feel that the other person is safe for us to express our emotions, and third, we must trust the other person in order to expose ourselves emotionally.

Our early evaluations of trust and safety based upon our cognitive and emotional processes during the early attachment process becomes wired in our brains at an early age. This is what Bowlby called the Internal Working Model.

Remember, Bowlby stated that our internal working model is the template that is formed during our attachment process that demonstrates that all intimate relationships in our lives are based upon the early relationship we formed with our primary caregiver during our early years of life.

We react and interact in our adult relationships in the manner that got programmed into our young brains while interacting with our primary caregiver. We often feel similar emotions. If our early relationship created anxiety, then we feel anxiety in our adult relationships. On the other hand, if our parents were able to form a strong, secure attachment with us when we were young, then we will feel confident and secure in connecting with another individual as an adult.

Our sense of security lies inside of our internal working model. The attachment process is intense, and it is a vital part of our identity as well as an imperative part of our behavior. Our identity begins to form in the womb. Attachment begins with conception. Another significant component of the attachment process is the biological component. During the period of pregnancy, the mother is the major provider for her child through taking care of her own physical needs and maintaining good health that the mother is delivering a message of love to her child. The child also receives the message of whether he/she is a wanted baby.

The birth process is supposed to be intentionally set up for the child to be welcomed into the world. Just as much as the child is receiving love, the welcoming and acceptance of the child brings love to the parents. At least, this is what is supposed to happen. The ideal connection between two human beings is the reciprocity of love, giving and receiving of love. The mother providing milk to her infant child through her breast creates a positive attachment that also creates safety and trust. The mother and child are becoming a unit. The mother and infant are creating a symbiotic relationship. The mother is becoming imprinted into the child's DNA.

Bruce Perry once said that the child's DNA is correlated with the child's environment and that the child's environment dictates the child's DNA. This begins with the birth process. This is the root of the biological makeup of a child. An infant receives his/her oxygen and nutrients through the umbilical cord. In addition, the umbilical cord is basically a lifeline between the mother and infant.

It is through this lifeline (umbilical cord) that the infant also receives messages that life is good or life is a struggle. This is the first time that Bowlby's bonding cycle, where trust is formed when basic needs are met. Unfortunately, it is also the foundation where attachment and trust can go awry. When pregnant mothers use alcohol or drugs, the alcohol and drugs get transmitted to the infant through the umbilical cord and usually causes significant damage to the infant's brain. The cry of a baby who is healthy is very different than the cry of an addicted baby or a baby who has been traumatized. The biological process can go positive or negative extremely similar to the cognitive and emotional processes of attachment.

When the biological process goes positive, along with the emotional and cognitive processes of attachment, then safety and trust are formed, and security is wired inside the child's internal working model. When the biological process goes awry, then the emotional and cognitive processes of attachment will most likely also go awry creating a lack of trust, a lack of safety and insecurity to be wired inside the child's internal working model.

As I incorporated the biological, cognitive, and emotional components of the attachment process, all of the components of attachment work together to create the internal working model. The only reason why I separated the individual components of attachment is to demonstrate to the reader the understanding of how each component has its individual purpose, responsibility, and actions.

However, it is the integration of all of the components that comprise the attachment process.

In addition to the biological, cognitive, and emotional components is the behavioral component of the attachment process. Here are some questions that can help to determine the assessment of attachment: Did the mother demonstrate during pregnancy that her child will be welcomed into the world? Was the child shown loving acts of trust and safety toward the child? Is the child being taken care of? Does each parent demonstrate a loving positive attitude toward the child? Does each parent spend significant time holding the child? Does the parent give the baby massages and gentle, loving touch? Does the parent play with the child? These last three questions demonstrate the behavioral component of the attachment process.

Since love is demonstrative and we were wired by God for positive touch, it would make sense that touch or the parent's behavior toward the child is a significant component of the attachment process. The parent's behavior toward the child is another component that could be either positive or negative. Remember, it is consistency not constancy that is the possibility and the goal.

Does the parent's behavior toward the child show a consistent pattern of positive interaction or a negative interaction with the child? A significant part of my dissertation studied how the parent's attitude plays a significant role in the success of that child. Children figure out their environment by collecting all the data from their parents, process it in their own ways, interpret the data and then often play out their interpretations of that data. Children are sponges to their environment. They soak in the data, interpret it and then often replicate their interpretations through their behavior.

A person's behavior reveals that individual's beliefs. A person's beliefs are often formed or created early on in life through our interpretations of significant events and often by the behaviors and attitudes of significant people in our lives. Children will not remember everything. However, children will always remember how important they are to the people whom were most important to them.

Children learn through their five senses, and they form their interpretations from the input of the data through their senses. So, another component of the attachment process is the sensory integration component. This refers to the five senses and how learning, especially for a child takes place through the integration of all of our senses. All of this information, this culmination of data collected from conception through the early years of life (age 6), is inputted into the brain almost like a computer program and the child's internal working model is created.

Hopefully, you are putting the puzzle together that the child's internal working model is the executive director for the child's beliefs and behaviors. This is why I believe that attachment is at the core foundation for most psychological pathology. When we have secure attachment, we have a strong positive internal working model with a high sense of security, which connects us to our essence. When we have a form of insecure attachment, we have a weak and struggling internal working model with a high sense of insecurity, which connects us to a false identity.

4

What Goes Wrong During the Attachment Process?

The majority of the previous chapter was focused on healthy or secure attachment. In this chapter, I will discuss the many negative elements that produce insecure attachment. There are different types of insecure attachment, which include: Preoccupied, Fearful, Dismissive, Disorganized. The scope of this book is not on the details of the typology of insecure attachment.

Rather, this book is focused on the role of attachment in the foundation for discovering our essence. I will continue to discuss the journey for discovering our essence. In the previous chapter, I discussed what attachment actually is and its role in our lives. Attachment is the executive director for our thoughts, emotions, and behavior. In this chapter, we will learn what goes wrong during the attachment process that causes us to have insecure attachment

Since, attachment begins at conception, what the mother takes into her body, such as alcohol or drugs has a vital role in creating insecure attachment. Remember, the umbilical cord is the infant's lifeline; therefore, whatever the mother is ingesting is being induced into the child's body and brain. One of the major components of the attachment process is the biological component. And biology plays a significant role in the conception and pregnancy stages of the child's life.

One significant factor at this stage is how well the mother is taking care of herself as well how well she is taking care of her child. When the mother uses alcohol or drugs, alcohol or drugs gets ingested by the infant. There is an immense amount of research on the topic of fetal alcohol syndrome and the significant amount of damage it causes.

Psychologists are still studying the effects of drug-induced infants. One of the symptoms that I have witnessed as well as discussed with adoptive mothers, is that right at birth the pitch of a crying drug-induced infant is far more startling and unsettling than a crying healthy infant. The drug induced infant also seems to give mixed signals to his or her mother when feeling distressed. For example, the drug induced infant will scream in her cry almost desperate to be held by mom and then when mom picks her up, she begins to be unsettled by being held as well. Children who have a difficult start in life through the trauma of being a drug induced infant, often have a struggle with becoming securely attached.

As I stated in an earlier chapter, a significant positive outcome of secure attachment is a child with the wiring to emotionally regulate in healthy ways. When there is any form of neglect or other types of child maltreatment, then the child is missing the wiring for the ability to emotionally regulate.

Later in life, the inability to self-regulate becomes most prevalent in romantic relationships. Romantic relationships are also the place where our primary relationship is most manifested. When our internal working model is mis-wired, we attempt to lean on our romantic partner or another individual who is significant to us, to regulate our emotions. We create a philosophy that says if so and so is doing well, I am doing well. When this same individual is emotionally distant from us, we are not okay. Due to our mis-wired internal working model, we struggle for ways to regulate our emotions and calm ourselves.

The womb is supposed to be a place of safety and refuge. Remember, safety comes before trust in the development of a close, loving, reciprocating relationship. In addition, we have been discussing how having our needs met transforms into trust. Infants have very basic logic wired in their brains. Input equals output. Drugs and chemicals that are poisonous to me are being forced into my system. The person who is doing this to my body and brain cannot be trusted. Hence, the attachment process for the child is blocked with mistrust and messages that mother is dangerous. The exact opposite message an infant need to receive.

Every single human being needs to receive a message that he or she is loved and that they can trust. Otherwise, life becomes one major obstacle after another. In addition, psychologists are trained to assess the impact of trauma by determining the age of onset for the trauma and by whom was the trauma caused by. For example, it is bad enough that a child was sexually abused at age three. But now imagine that the abuser is the child's parent. Now, that is a deeper trauma based upon the age of onset coupled with the relationship to the abuser is the child's parent, which is the very person whom the child needs to trust in order to have a mentally healthy life.

Trust is one of the most imperative goals of the attachment process, especially during pregnancy and the first year of life. Our lives are fully dependent upon our mothers at this point of time. Trust is earned over time through consistent acts of meeting one's needs. Trust is earned by being nurtured in a positive manner that is never exploited.

Trust is earned by being able to depend upon someone else who shows reliability and concern. Trust is also earned by the other person genuinely concerned about your welfare. The challenge is that there are numerous trials of earning trust throughout the day and no individual is going to get it right every single time. However, during the embryo stage, our quality of life is fully dependent upon how well our mothers take care of us in the womb.

Babies form a significant bond to their mothers during pregnancy. There are a lot of changes and transitions during the embryo stage, which is preparing us for the birth process. Some attachment specialists state that the birth process can predict a lot of future behavior, beliefs, and attitudes.

One of the things that I have noticed is that mothers who have children exhibiting attention deficit disorder in their early academic years often state that their pregnancy was filled with stress and anxiety. Another thing that I have noticed is the time of day that we were born seems to be correlated with the peak time of our daily performance. Other correlations include caesarean-section babies usually have difficulty as adults being on time for appointments.

What happens during our birth process will not be remembered in the cognitive part of our memory. However, there is research that what often happens is our birth process is remembered in our bodies, our cellular makeup. It becomes wired in our senses and executes our natural response to touch.

Our birth process becomes hard-wired in our Internal Working Model. This is because our birth process is the second stage of our attachment process. Our birth process is probably the most drastic transition in life. Individuals who are securely attached will transition much more successfully during major changes in their life than individuals who are insecurely attached. Our birth process can be scary, leading us to feelings of fear and anxiety later in life.

There can be physical and medical complications that can go wrong during the birth process. Obviously, this will induce fear for the mother, child, and perhaps everyone involved in the birth process, including doctors and nurses. We are discussing another significant element of the biological component of attachment. This might sound outrageous to some of you. However, there is a vital body of research that expresses that the body receives and stores messages like love, safety, nurturance, harm.

These messages also become wired into our Internal Working Model, the executive director for our behavior, thoughts, and emotions. Ultimately, our time in utero and our birth process becomes wired in our Internal Working Model and we acquire a foundation where we learn to relate to the world through our messages received during these chapters of our lives.

The next chapter of our lives is the period of time where we are fully dependent upon our parents or primary caregiver. I sometimes look at a baby with awe and wonder what is this little person thinking. How do they see the world? But then comes the conclusion that their entire world is strictly all about being taken care of or Start

If the baby is being taken care of and nurtured during his/her first year of life, then he/she will feel safe and trust his/her caregivers and his/her world. If he/she does not feel safe, he/she learns that his/her caregivers are not trustworthy, and he/she does not feel safe.

The inability to learn to trust and feel safe during their first year of life often is the root of pathology that is associated with the attachment process. For example, the person who acquires the antisocial personality disorder in adulthood has been on a journey of destructiveness since their first year of life. The etiology (root) of antisocial personality disorder is pathological severe neglect. The symptomology of the antisocial personality disorder consists of no positive regard for others, a lack of empathy (understanding the feelings of others), often a lack of emotions, consistent trouble with the law, often committing acts of violence, and a lack of remorse. Often, these same individuals were diagnosed as having conduct disorder in their teenage years and prior to their teen years, were diagnosed with oppositional defiant disorder.

Attachment experts would probably diagnose this same individual as someone with reactive attachment disorder or disorganized attachment disorder. I consider these two types of insecure attachment as the most concerning of all the attachment disorders. Some attachment experts state that there are two types of reactive attachment disorder: Inhibited (withdrawal, sadness) and Disinhibited (acting out).

I believe that Reactive Attachment Disorder is the least common form of the attachment styles. I also believe that the true criteria for Reactive Attachment Disorder is that the child has no conscience or at minimum behaves in a manner that shows a lack of conscience, such as demonstrating no positive regard toward others, a lack of empathy, a willingness to cause harm to others, lying, stealing, having no positive relationships, withdrawal or rebelliousness from others, no respect for authority, and appears fearless. This individual is also at high risk for becoming a future criminal, if not already participating in criminal acts.

The other concerning attachment style, besides the Reactive Attachment Disorder is the Disorganized Attachment style. Mary Main derived this term from her research in attachment, studying mothers attempting to comfort their young children. Main found that there was a group of mothers who appeared to do everything right in their attempt to meet their child's need and desire to be comforted when the child was distressed and yet the child also appeared to be fearful of their mother's care.

Main coined the term Disorganized Attachment based on this ambivalence between the mother and child. As Main investigated, she discovered that each of these mothers had a challenging childhood and never became securely attached in their childhoods. I have discussing throughout this book, that attachment is internal, not external attaching to people or to things. Rather, as Bowlby stated attachment creates an Internal Working Model. The mothers who were creating a Disorganized Attachment Style with their children had a very poor Internal Working Model and insecure attachment, probably a disorganized style as well.

It is not that attachment styles are a destiny. Main also discovered that this same group of mothers had never been to therapy and had never resolved their internal attachment challenges and issues. While mothers who had resolved their internal attachment patterns were able to create a secure attachment pattern with their children.

The children who developed the disorganized attachment style had grave difficulty staying out of trouble. Children with disorganized attachment disorder appear to act out with others their internal chaos, ambivalence and contradictory patterns of safety and security. For example, this particular child will tend to mistreat his or her friends. This child can be very superficially and charming, and then a short time later be deceitful and hurtful toward the very person who was being nice to them. This child's behavior ends to match the criteria for oppositional defiant disorder or even conduct disorder.

He/She has difficulty maintaining friendships over time. And this child will tend to act in very annoying ways toward both their peers as well as toward parents and teachers.

When I have counseled these children, I have found that the majority of these children are actually intelligent, talented, and thoughtful children who act in annoying and hurtful manners that are motivated out of fear. Out of all the individuals that I have treated, counseled, taught, or interacted with, I have found this particular individual to most closely show how their essence has gotten buried out of their badly wired Internal Working Model that is filled with messages stating that the others cannot be trusted, and the world is an unsafe place.

I have also found that many of these children have the potential to be future leaders if they were able to trust their teachers and allowed them to actually educate them to their fullest potential.

I wrote my dissertation on the influence of the parent's internal attachment patterns on their elementary school children's academic performance and found that there is strong correlation between the security inside of a parent and the security they create on the outside of themselves with their children. In the previous paragraphs, I discussed how disorganized attachment disorder is created from the parent's unresolved trauma and the parent's mis-wired Internal Working Model.

Again, the child with disorganized attachment disorder is like a role-model or prototype that fits the description of how Internal Working Models get passed onto the next generation.

There are two additional types of insecure attachment that are created by the actions of the primary caregivers. These are the Avoidant or Dismissive Attachment style and the Anxious-Ambivalent or Preoccupied Attachment Style.

I believe that Beverly James said it best when she stated that the Avoidant or Dismissive Attachment Style is created from a child being neglected by his/her parents on a consistent and regular basis. This individual, due to his or her neglect in childhood, is strictly not interested in relationships and finds no value in relationships. Beverly James also states that the Anxious-Ambivalent or Preoccupied Attachment Individual has a history of abuse.

This makes a lot of sense. The individual with Anxious Ambivalence has experienced relationship and wishes for a healthy relationship, but often experiences high levels of anxiety due to his or her past experiences of abusive relationships, often starting from his or her primary caregiver. Sadly, this individual often repeats the pattern of attempting to have a relationship with an abusive partner.

Remember, our Internal Working Model needs to be rewired with healthy patterns and healthy messages in order to 1) Discover our essence, and 2) Create Healthy Relationships. Both individuals are prone to sabotage good loving relationships because they feel deep down that they can't trust and that there is no real love for them.

As you are learning, our Internal Working Models are the executors of our behaviors, thoughts, and emotions.

Our Internal Working Models are also at the foundation of our emotional wounds experienced early in life. One huge positive manifestation of discovering our essence is to rewire our Internal Working Model so that our Internal Working Model matches or aligns with our essence.

Other manifestations of poor attachment and mis-wired Internal Working Models are pathology, including personality disorders. I will discuss the two most prevalent personality disorders in our society, Narcissism and Borderline Personality Disorder.

There is research that shows that there is a correlation between poor or insecure attachment and borderline personality disorder. Individuals who exhibit symptoms of borderline personality disorder also show signs of the preoccupied or anxious-ambivalent attachment style. This individual is seeking love and at the same time does not believe he or she can find love.

One of the challenges for the person with Borderline Personality Disorder is that he or she often self-sabotages almost every aspect of their life. I have found that subconsciously, the individual with borderline personality disorder engages in an intense conflict with people they are closest to in order to determine if they are important enough to fight with. If the other person engages in the argument with the person who has borderline personality disorder, then they believe they are important to the other person, but if the other person refuses to engage in the argument, then the person with borderline personality disorder feels rejected and abandoned.

One of the criteria traits that is at the root of Borderline Personality Disorder is the feeling of abandonment. During the early years of an individual with Borderline Personality Disorder is the experience of being abandoned either emotionally or physically. Either the parent of this individual has left them for good or this individual has had their emotional security shattered.

Abuse from a primary caregiver toward a child, especially sexual abuse, can leave a child's emotional security shattered. Children think in very black and white terms and very concrete terms. Children interpret the behavior of others toward them as being about them, me the child. My parents are abusing me because I am bad or I deserve it. When a child lacks safety in his or her life, the child often feels alone in the world.

This child who grows up in an abusive household during his or her first three years of life also has grown up in a chaotic environment. Remember, we bring our Internal Working Model with us everywhere we go. This individual has chaos wired into his or her Internal Working Model who then manifests chaos into his or her personal relationships. Often, individuals who exhibit borderline traits will also demonstrate chaos by creating illogical conflicts with a lot of anger and sometimes aggression. This individual can even become violent and dangerous. Another common trait is rage.

The Internal Working Model of an individual with Borderline Personality Disorder is wired with chaos, irrational/illogical beliefs about love, mistrust, viewing the world as unsafe, and a lot of hurt and anger. The individual who exhibits borderline traits also demonstrates feeling unsafe, mistrusting, often interprets any form of ambiguous statements as negative and hurtful and is easily triggered.

We will discuss how triggers work in more detail in a later chapter. For now, I want to explain that a trigger is a switch that connects our interpretation of a statement or event with an emotion. And our interpretations of events and statements are linked to our experiences in our past.

Since, the individual with borderline personality disorder has a significant history of hurt and anger, many if not most of the ambiguous messages sent to an individual with borderline personality disorder will be interpreted as hurtful statements.

When an individual has a history and Internal Working Model filled with chaos, hurt, anger, unresolved traumas, mistrust, unsafety, and a very insecure foundation, this individual will also be at very high risk of going into rage attacks. A rage attack is often a dissociative act where the individual has been triggered to the point of manifesting a major meltdown with an adult temper-tantrum.

During this rage attack, it is very possible to become violent without any intention to be violent, almost like the Hulk. After the rage attack, the individual with borderline personality disorder can look at the person he or she just attacked as if there is something wrong with the other person. He or she might not even be aware of what was said or done during the rage attack.

The individual with borderline personality disorder switches moods quickly, often going from anger to laughter, to calmness within minutes. This also leaves his or her partner very confused. I often tell individuals who are involved with someone with borderline personality disorder that they can feel as if he or she has left a tornado experience of emotions with no logical conclusion of what was said or occurred.

The individual with borderline personality disorder lacks self-awareness and often appears to act in manners like the traits of being dissociative. Their emotions are very intense. They can appear to act very childish and even appear crazy to many individuals. This individual has grave difficulty maintaining long-term friendships and relationships.

It becomes emotionally exhausting to be with an individual with borderline personality disorder because of their emotional instability, moving one emotion to the next quickly, and because of their intense emotions and lack of logic. These individual likes to have people view them as intelligent and so they make up stuff thinking that they are sounding smart when they sound foolish and immature.

In addition to acting immature and aggressive, the individual with borderline personality disorder can also act very flirtatious. Often, she/he has an intensive sexual history with numerous partners. She/he with borderline personality disorder believes that the only thing that another person would be interested in is spending time with her/his body. She/he is willing to give up her/his body in exchange for a temporary high of feeling wanted and maybe loved. However, her/his subconscious motive is to re-create her or his early trauma and end up feeling abandoned.

Individuals who struggle with borderline personality disorder struggle with socialization. Usually, when there is a group situation, the individual with borderline traits will attempt to charm the leader of that particular group in an attempt to be in control, avoid abandonment, and be in a position of envy from others.

Another complex oddity of socialization with individuals with borderline traits is that they have grave difficulty socializing in threes. The individual with borderline traits will either withdraw and act out his or her abandonment issues or this individual will attempt to divide and conquer, making one person bad and the other person her best friend. Another possible scenario is where the individual with borderline traits will act out in front of both individuals in order to gain attention and concern from both individuals.

Another attention getting tactic, which is dangerous, is attempting to gain attention through cries of suicide. Many psychologists believe that individuals with borderline traits really do not want to attempt suicide. Rather, they can be filled with suicidal ideation, meaning that he or she will feel as if his or her life has no meaning, no hope, and no interest to anyone. However, most do not go through with the suicide attempt. This does not mean that we should not take them seriously. We need to take every individual's cry of suicide seriously. Individuals with borderline personality disorder are lonely individuals with a desperate cry for connection with others.

The challenge is that the individual with borderline personality disorder becomes enmeshed with the person whom he/she feels closest to. Enmeshment refers to being so emotionally close as to desiring that the other person feels exactly what he/she feels at the exact moment he/she is experiencing those emotions. This is impossible to do. However, the individual with borderline personality disorder basically demands it to happen. When it doesn't happen, which is inevitable, the individual with borderline personality disorder often feels abandoned and often goes into a rage.

This is one of the huge challenges why others have grave difficulty maintain any type of relationship for a length of time with an individual with borderline traits. Other grave difficult obstacles for the individual with borderline traits in a relationship include a lack of empathy and seeing others as all good until they become all bad. This individual is often emotionally two years old.

Two-year olds do not know have the understanding that other people have emotions and struggles. A typical two-year old child sees others as an extension of themselves and are there to provide for the needs of the individual with borderline traits. So, a person with strong borderline traits views the individual that they feel closest to as all knowing, all powerful, and that there are no struggles or problems for this individual. In addition, the individual with borderline traits views their soulmate as someone who only has positive emotions (joy all the time).

The soulmate cannot be angry or sad or struggling. The soulmate is there to serve the individual with borderline traits. When the soulmate expresses his true emotions or demonstrates imperfections to the individual with borderline traits; the individual with borderline traits makes the soulmate bad and attempts to scold the soulmate usually through some type of passive aggressive act of withdrawing from the relationship and not speaking to the soulmate.

One of the traits that becomes very confusing to the soulmate is 1) often there is no explanation from the individual with borderline traits about her behavior, 2) after a short period of time, the individual with borderline traits will act as if there is nothing wrong. I have often coached soulmates into understanding that the soulmate will have to understand that the individual with borderline traits will act very differently over short periods of time, almost as if having multiple personalities. I use the expression, you never know who you are going to meet today, even though it is the same person.

This is why I strongly believe that many individuals who are being diagnosed with bi-polar disorder actually have borderline personality disorder. Bi-Polar is a term thrown around a lot by the public whenever someone changes his or her moods quickly. Bi-Polar is a complex biological disorder that is actually mush more rare than present-day diagnosis. However, borderline personality disorder is much more common than what many want you to believe.

Since, we are aligning Internal Working Models and Attachment Styles to pathology, including personality disorders, I will offer an easy explanation to the popularity of personality disorders in our society. With the significantly increasing rate of early childhood trauma in our society, we will also see a significantly increasing rate of insecure attachment styles, especially the disorganized attachment style and the preoccupied (anxious ambivalent) style. The connection is that individuals with borderline traits will fall into one of these two categories (preoccupied/anxious-ambivalent or disorganized).

Earlier. I briefly discussed some of the traits of the preoccupied or anxious-ambivalent attachment style. Now, let s get a better understanding of this Internal Working Model for the individual who has borderline personality disorder and has the preoccupied attachment style.

A summary of characteristics or symptoms of borderline personality disorder include: a high degree of anxiety, often rage, often depression, a strong desire to be taken care of emotionally (some refer to this as enmeshment), challenges with all types of relationships, severe fluctuation of mood (this is where people think bi-polar), sometimes flirtatious, sometimes promiscuous, often putting a spin to what was said (twisting what someone said), often feeling hurt, often feeling abandoned, viewing self as a victim, wanting to punish others, usually creating drama, fearful of peaceful times, in need of constant attention, often causing strife amongst others, sometimes obsessed with suicidal ideation, and often wanting to be viewed upon by others as knowledgeable and intelligent.

Here is a summary of preoccupied attachment style: severe anxiety, often feeling alone or abandoned, believing that they have to lose something, such as giving into sex, giving money or favors in order to gain being liked, often annoying others maintaining relationships, needing constant attention, often jealous, and believing that no one likes them. Do you see similarities between a person with borderline personality disorder and a person with preoccupied attachment style?

My point is that personality disorders are linked to attachment styles. Another example is the correlation between the dismissive or avoidant personality disorder and the narcissistic personality disorder. A typical trait of narcissism is the belief that he or she does not need anything from anyone. The narcissistic individual sees people as a nuisance and very little to gain from a relationship. When an individual with narcissism is involved in a relationship, it is because the other person needs them. An individual with narcissism sees him/herself as a hero, a rescuer, someone who is needed to make another person valuable.

Individuals who struggle with narcissism do not view their partners as equals. Rather, narcissistic individuals view their partners as people who should praise and admire them. In addition, narcissistic individuals do not really respect their partners. Narcissistic individuals view their partners as individuals who are fortunate to have them in their lives. So, the narcissistic individual is seeking a partner who has low self-esteem, struggles with self-identity, and looks to a partner for self-identity. I just gave a very brief description of borderline personality disorder. The term borderline personality disorder means on the border of having a personality, an identity, which was discussed earlier.

Often, the narcissistic individual and the borderline individual become attracted to each other unaware of the motives mentioned in the previous paragraph. The narcissistic individual is enthralled that he has found someone who sees him as God, all knowing, all powerful, and can do anything. The borderline individual is excited that she has found someone that she can brag about and occupies her time and her mind. Thus, the individual with dismissive attachment style and the individual with preoccupied personality disorder are attracted to each other.

This creates an interesting psychological and emotional dance for the two of them as well as for those observing this relationship. The individual with narcissism sees himself as being the rescuer in the relationship, the partner who is always solving all the problems and always providing. The individual with borderline personality disorder sees herself in the beginning of the relationship as the one who is being rescued and being taken care of.

As the relationship evolves, she will see herself as the victim, the one being used for sexual purposes, the one who is being used in emotional ways. The individual with borderline personality will also see herself as being forgotten, abused emotionally, and will be filled with anxiety due to uncertainty of her role and value in the relationship.

The individual with narcissism will never allow himself to be vulnerable in any way. The individual with narcissism hates being wrong, out of control or looking foolish to anyone. So, this individual works very hard at only showing what they are actually know as well as showing only their actual talents. They will never risk being wrong or appearing to be bad, foolish, or incapable. This individual will never place themselves in a position of risk, especially if others know about their ventures. For example, the child with narcissism will not participate unless he knows he is going to look smart, talented, or admired. If there is any doubt, he will not participate. This evolves and continues into adulthood.

As a narcissistic adult, he will date and marry only the people who he thinks draws attention from the crowd. The narcissistic adult will only perform at tasks where he is most likely going to be praised and admired for his performance, whether it be work or play. This individual will also only say things that he actually knows and can be backed up. The narcissistic individual does not take risks if the risks involve any potential of appearing foolish, dumb, or inadequate in any way. This individual also works very hard at never being open with his feelings or thoughts. This individual is very much living out of his façade.

Where did the façade originate? Like most psychological and emotional issues, the façade of narcissism originated in early childhood. Many times, a narcissistic parent will raise a narcissistic child who develops into a narcissistic adult. Another way that parents manifest narcissism in their child is through consistent acts of denying their child's misbehavior, blaming others for the mistakes their child makes, attempting to make others think that their child is perfect, and consistently giving messages to their child about how they are better than everyone else. It is one thing to give your child positive attention. It is entirely different to give your child stupid messages like, you can do anything you set your mind to. That is a stupid statement because that is false for every one of us. And another way that narcissism can become manifested is through a child's perception and beliefs that he or she is the healthy one in the family.

Personality disorders are created in our childhoods within the context of our families. Yes, even though our personality is still developing and evolving. If you know what you are looking at as well as knowing what you are listening to, you can detect narcissism or borderline personality disorder in young individuals. Some psychologists say that all teenagers are narcissistic. First, this is most definitely not true. Second, there is a huge difference between an individual who has narcissistic traits and an individual with narcissistic personality disorder.

The internal working model of the individual who has narcissistic personality disorder consists of covering up shame, covering up or hiding mistakes, attempting to shine or be the star in any situation, exaggerating achievements, accomplishments, and exaggerating self-importance. This individual's internal working model is a huge façade of lies covering a lot of shame and fear that he doesn't and won't measure up.

When we live out of our essence, we accept the fact that all of us are inadequate. It is the way God created us on purpose. Why? So, that we are humble and accept our dependence upon God. True emotional and spiritual maturity is the acceptance of our limitations, mistakes, and talents. We accept that we have and will make mistakes. We accept that we are gifted in specific ways and not gifted in everything.

We understand that God created every individual to be interdependent not independent. We are living out of our essence when we can admit our limitations and our mistakes in a very matter of fact manner. We are living out of our essence when we can accept our value and when we accept our talents, our intelligence, and our true abilities. We accept all of ourselves in a very matter of fact manner when we are living out of our essence. I have been instructing you on understanding that trauma creates a mis-wired internal working model.

A mis-wired internal working model is demonstrated when an individual cannot see his/her value. This individual often goes through life as not achieving all the things that God has for that induvial to accomplish. Why doesn't this individual accomplish these things? It is not because they do not have the talent. It is not because they lack the intelligence, it is also not because this person is lazy.

Rather, this individual places obstacles in his path without recognizing he is doing this. It is this subconscious attitude that gets manifested in negative thinking. This individual, because of his poor self-esteem, presents himself in a negative way. Without us doing it intentionally, we often present ourselves in negative ways through our speech, our withdrawal from others, and our behaviors that make others doubt our abilities. It is like an internal mirror. Often, others see us according to our internal messages and our internal beliefs about ourselves. The mis-wired internal working model becomes evident to others without anyone being aware that this is what is occurring.

Another manifestation of a mis-wired internal working model is when an individual is expressing arrogance or narcissism. Trauma and poor parenting can create narcissism. We discussed narcissism earlier in this chapter. This individual is fighting and working hard at covering up his or her shame. These individuals attempt to attack others before he or she receives any negative attention. These individuals are also quick to attack anyone who attempts to expose their mistakes or character of the individual with narcissism. The narcissistic individual works hard at always shining (being the star). This individual is extremely self-absorbed and everything that this individual is involved with creates some type of investment, whether financial, status, power, or flattery.

As you are learning, our true internal working model is not invested in show, attention-seeking, covering up shame, or in holding our heads low and not valuing ourselves. Each of our healthy internal working models is rooted in humility, acceptance of our talents, and acceptance of what we are not gifted in. A healthy internal working model also consists of peace, love, security, and healthy mental wellness.

Again, a healthy internal working model consists of healthy self-esteem. We recognize and accept what we are capable of, what we have to work hard at, and what we are limited in doing. I have worked with numerous parents who want their children to be someone whom they are not.

The parents I am talking about tell their children lies. These lies have a theme. Telling the child that he or she is good at something they have limited talent at best. Also, downplaying what the child is truly good at. A lot of these types of parents attempt to live vicariously through their children. If a parent couldn't make it as a football player when he was young, this dad will push football on his son when the son has limited talent and little interest in playing football.

A parent who couldn't or did not fulfill his/her dreams and goals will attempt to push his or her child into areas of life that the child was never designed to do. The perfect scenario is when a parent raises up a child according to whom that child is meant to become. Most parents do not know how to do this. Another purpose of this book is to help parents heal and to help parents guide their children to become self-actualized, the person that God created them to become. This is how I define essence.

So, most individuals lose their discovery of their essence in the early years of their lives. Therefore, they also create a mis-wired internal working model. The unfortunate reality is that most individuals live their entire lives out of their mis-wired internal working models, never discovering their essence.

We have been discussing different ways that a mis-wired internal working model becomes created. I explained the two most popular personality disorders and their connection to two of the attachment styles. I also explained how trauma impacts our essence and our internal working models. I have been discussing early childhood trauma because this is the most challenging to endure as a human being and early childhood trauma has the most impact upon our internal working model.

So, what other ways can cause attachment to go astray. Let's first look at the different categories of trauma. Trauma can include child abuse (physical, sexual, emotional, and verbal), neglect, abandonment, coming from divorced parents, growing up with parents with addictions, being adopted, and being rejected are just some of the different traumas people can experience.

Other traumas can include growing up with a mentally ill parent or guardian, growing up with a parent who suffers with PTSD, growing up with a parent who is physically ill often or having a serious physical illness yourself or having a mental illness yourself. It would take numerous pages to list all the different traumas. I define trauma as an event that you have experienced that has caused a strong negative response within yourself. Trauma does not compute for any of us, especially a young child. Trauma has our thoughts going in circles without a conclusion or an ending, like a gerbil on a treadmill.

One of the biggest challenges is attempting to make sense out of our trauma. Trauma fragments the brain in ways that makes it difficult to concentrate, to focus, to be at peace with our selves, to be at peace with the world, to listen, to maintain positive perceptions, to have healthy self-esteem, to be able to problem-solve, to maintain positive cash flow. Trauma affects all aspects of our lives. In addition, as I have stated numerous times already, it impacts negatively our internal working model through poor attachment.

Individuals with poor attachment patterns and mis-wired internal working models are attracted to other individuals who have poor attachment patterns and mis-wired internal working models. Earlier, I discussed the dance between the individual with narcissism and the individual with borderline personality disorder.

Wounded individuals are subconsciously attracted to other wounded individuals because we think that we found our refuge. The refuge that wounded individuals often seek is that of understanding and often a place to rest in the bosom of someone who has experienced similar trauma. All of us have a strong internal desire to be seen, to be heard, and to be understood. Most wounded individuals have an internal desire to escape from life with only one other person and that person is someone that can comfort us out of the need to be comforted. This creates a very dysfunctional unsatisfactory relationship that is based on a foundation of trauma.

Two dysfunctional individuals with mis-wired internal working models become attracted to each other in hopes of being rescued from their pain. Over time, each becomes resentful and bitter toward the other for causing them more pain, rarely recognizing that the attraction was based on wounds and dysfunction. Now, if these two dysfunctional individuals with mis-wired internal working models have children. The children will have mis-wired internal working models.

Mary Main (1988) discovered that mothers who were tending to their children's distress could still create poor attachment patterns within their children due to their mis-wired internal working model. Several research studies conducted by Main (1988) showed that there was a group of mothers who could not ease their infant's distress in spite that this same group of mothers followed all the nurturing steps that would normally ease an infant's distress. Rather, the children were ambivalent, fluctuating between wanting to be comforted and being fearful of their primary caregiver. The ambivalence demonstrated by the infants motivated Main to coin the term, disorganized attachment patterns.

Disorganized attachment disorder sets the stage of a very challenging life. Children with disorganized attachment pattern misbehave and get into trouble on a consistent basis. These children have grave difficulty maintaining healthy positive friendships, often annoying the people around them. Children with disorganized attachment pattern have tumultuous relationships with their parents and other family members. And, these children often grow into teens and young adults who fall prey to committing crimes, addictions, poor relationships, going to jail, and usually being underemployed.

The description above reveals the internal working model of the individual with disorganized attachment pattern. In addition, this individual with disorganized attachment pattern suffers with low self-esteem, poor self-image, and internal messages that sounds like No one loves me. It becomes obvious that this same individual with disorganized attachment pattern has his/her essence buried.

The path of healing for the individual with disorganized attachment pattern is therapy and focusing on re-parenting. This individual is the recipient of a parent's unresolved trauma. Parents have a lot of power and tremendous influence to create either a healthy positive internal working model within her or his child or to create a mis-wired internal working model within his or her child. One of the greatest gifts a parent can give to his or her child is a mentally healthy parent who parents in healthy ways.

5

Existential Aloneness

What is existential aloneness and why are we discussing it here?

Existentialism is the philosophical study of the meaning of existence. Philosophers such as Kierkegaard, Descartes, Nietzsche, Goethe, and Camu are just some of the greats who studied and examined the complexity of the human being and our search for meaning. Why are we here has been the most complex and most examined question from the beginning of time. One of the complexities of this study is that it cannot be examined without integrating one's spiritual beliefs.

At the foundational core of our essence is a belief in God. All of us are spiritual beings. It is our experiences, especially our trauma that causes our disbelief in God. Trauma causes us to view God in very similar patterns that were created by our parents or caregivers. For example, if we were abused in childhood, we will believe that God is an angry God or someone who cannot be trusted.

It is far more challenging for an individual who comes from an abusive home to have faith than for an individual who comes from a safe, loving, nurturing household. Our internal working model that is supposed to contain our essence and a deep connection with God becomes a mis-wired internal working model that contains a wounded sense of self filled with mistrust and anxiety.

We form our beliefs about God from our experiences in life, including our attachment patterns, our traumas, and our good experiences as well. This is why most of us have very ambivalent feelings about God. Religion is man's way of attempting to make sense out of his/her beliefs about God.

Existentialism crosses into the boundaries of every religion and spiritual belief there is, including agnostic beliefs and atheist beliefs. One simply cannot examine the meaning of life without having to come to some determination of one's understanding of creation. Thus, when we begin to examine creation, we are forced to determine our spiritual beliefs. The same is true when we begin to examine the purpose of human existence. We question our deepest emotions including loneliness and the relationship between emotions and human connection.

Human connection is a vital aspect of mental wellness. The manner in which we form or don't form human connections in our lives is rooted in our internal working models. A healthy internal working model will attract others with a healthy internal working model. And a mis-wired internal working model will attract others with mis-wired internal working models. Like begets like. We look for mirrors in others so that we have validation of our beliefs about ourselves and the world. We find conflict when we don't receive that validation.

Existential aloneness is described as the realization of our emotional disconnection from other human beings. It is the realization that we are alone in the world among seven billion other individuals who are also alone in the world. Aloneness does not necessarily bring on loneliness. It is a paradox to discover that the more one can acknowledge his or her aloneness, the more one has the ability to connect on a deep emotional level.

This paradox becomes true when one recognizes that other individuals will not be able to feel exactly what we are feeling. Empathy is not feeling another individual's feelings. Rather, empathy is being able to understand someone's experience and why he/she would be feeling the way he/she is feeling. Aloneness also means that we understand that no one knows our thoughts. Children, due to their egocentrism, expect others to know their thoughts and emotions. Mentally well individuals do not have this expectation and accepts that thoughts and emotions need to be expressed.

When we are living out of our essence and a healthy internal working model, we accept our reality and we strive to understand another individual s reality. I believe this is the ultimate in human connection and absolutely necessary in resolving any type of emotional conflict. A healthy internal working model does not need to engage in a power struggle over whose reality is valid and whose is not.

A healthy internal working model is seeking connection not enmeshment. When we seek connection, we seek to understand as well as to be understood. Healthy internal working models understand that listening is imperative in order to find understanding. You cannot understand someone's soul if you did not hear what he/she said. Connection happens when each person listens attentively to each other and each feels understood.

Enmeshment happens when there is a one-sided relationship where an individual is seeking to be nurtured by another individual on a consistent level. Enmeshment can also occur when an individual is attempting to find his purpose through constantly taking care of another individual emotionally without any desire for reciprocation.

Relationships need reciprocation in order to survive. Without reciprocation, one or both individuals will experience resentment, anger, sadness, abandonment, and feeling used. Individuals with healthy internal working models engage in healthy relationships that becomes a dance of nurturing each other without the need to nurture each other. Healthy internal working models want to nurture and be nurtured.

Individuals with mis-wired internal working models either seek to be in charge in the relationship or they seek to be taken care of by a nurturer. The individual who seeks to be in charge has grave difficulty trusting, most likely due to some unresolved feelings of being abandoned and counters his/her feelings with the need for others to depend upon him/her. The reason for the desire to have others depend upon you is the desire to not be abandoned as well as the desire to get all his/her needs met through domination. The individual who seeks to be taken care of is seeking to relive a happy childhood. Both individuals are having grave difficulty with facing their wounds and grieving their losses and pain.

When these individuals get together in a relationship, there is a lot of arguments. The unfortunate thing is both individuals are unaware of their subconscious desires and their wounds and often just play them out in their adult relationship. This creates a lot of havoc, arguments, sometimes violence, sometimes infidelity and a very strongly dysfunctional relationship. And all of this pain is rooted in each of their childhoods and manifested through each of their mis-wired internal working models.

If each of these individuals go through therapy for several months, sometimes years; they will discover in themselves a healthy internal working model wired to relate to another healthy internal working model. The ultimate purpose is to heal thyself and then others.

When we discover our essence and acquire a healthy internal working model, we become secure in ourselves and enter into relationships that will be healthy. I cannot believe that any relationship created out of infidelity or need for escape will be a healthy relationship. I cannot also believe that a relationship based upon the need to make up for loss or our wounds can be a healthy relationship. Healthy individuals attract other healthy individuals.

When healthy individuals discover their sense of internal emotional security, they also discover their healthy desires. Healthy internal working models create plans for their desires, such as playing sports, learning to play an instrument, attending college, traveling, and tending to other adventures. The mis-wired internal working model will avoid attempting such things, unless somehow talked into believing that they will be taken care of. The individual with a healthy internal working model is accepting of not being understood and their aloneness.

What happens internally when the individual with a mis-wired internal working model does not feel understood? Most of you have heard the saying the loneliest place to be is in a crowd. Have you ever noticed that when you are feeling lonely that feeling does not go away just because you are with people? The feeling only goes away when either we feel understood by others and thus connected or we understand that we have to acquire a connection internally, relying upon our own internalized secure infrastructure system.

Most of you have heard of the concept that it is easy to hide in a group. What makes this concept true? The challenge of being seen, being understood, and acquiring connection is what makes this concept true. Communication can be challenging. The same word can mean very different things to different people. Individuals react to words, actions, and concepts differently. Thus, there is an emotional wrestling that sometimes needs to happen between two individuals, in order for an emotional connection to happen.

It is through this emotional wrestling that old wounds are re-visited, and sometimes new wounds are created. However, it is also through this emotional wrestling that individuals really become vulnerable. And it is each individual's vulnerability that creates an emotionally intimate connection. This requires two people are willing to be vulnerable and who are willing to take the risk of being understood or not being understood.

One of the major differences I see between introverts and extroverts is that introverts seem to be more willing to be vulnerable than extroverts. Introverts are also more interested in having a deep intimate connection than extroverts. This becomes interesting to observe mainly because it is the extroverts who love to be around people and to be in groups. And it is the introverts who find people difficult to be around and do not enjoy group activities and yet want to philosophize about life and to share heavy intellectual thoughts and discussion. Introverts feel emotionally and often physically tired after being with people. Extroverts feel wired and excited when they are around people.

So how do extroverts and introverts interact in groups? We will first discuss group dynamics. In a group setting, there is seldom any deep discussion and it is seldom that individuals risk being vulnerable. This does not apply to self-help groups or to group therapy, where the objective is to be vulnerable. Take a look at the dynamics at a party. What do people talk about at a party? How much mingling goes on rather than having a one to one discussion about the problems in the world or the problems in their own home?

The structure is different in these types of group settings. Most individuals enter into a social setting with an internal agenda that usually fits that particular setting. Some individuals enter a party scene to meet someone for a date or even a one-night stand. Others enter a party scene to become the center of the party. And still others enter a party scene to forget about life for a few hours.

Introverts enter into a one to one relationship with the hopes of finding an emotional connection. The language is also different between introverts and extroverts because the thinking is vastly different. Introverts will want an emotionally intimate connection while extroverts want to have fun and enjoy themselves.

So, we connect through language that is used in order to attempt to reach our emotional goal at that moment. I do not believe that introversion or extroversion comes out of trauma nor a mis-wired internal working model. I do believe that how we utilize our introversion and extroversion traits in a relationship, especially when we first approach an individual we do not know, comes from our internal working models.

Mentally well individuals with healthy internal working models approach strangers in a friendly but cautions manner. The healthy internal working model attempts to gather as much information as they share. The healthy internal working model also understands that there are often numerous ways to interpret a specific event and numerous ways to interpret communication. Individuals with a lot of unresolved trauma, especially the individual who struggles with borderline personality disorder insists that their interpretation is the only interpretation.

Individuals with healthy internal working models focus on adjusting or tuning their internal world in order to adjust to the present situation. While the individual with a mis-wired internal working model attempts to control their external world and their focus is on others. Jean Paul Sarte calls this anguish when an individual is struggling to change his or her external world in order to match his or her internal thoughts and emotions.

Remember, the individual with a healthy internal working model is also an individual who has discovered his or her essence. This individual with secure attachment does not desire nor attempts to change his or her external world. Rather, this individual focuses on tuning his or her internal world to be able to adjust to his or her external world. When we know who we are we can sit in other people's circles without the fear of having to change nor determine who is right..

6

Grief and Loss:

Why would I bring this chapter and topic into this book? I give credit to my friend, Shannon Dunnan, for this chapter. Shannon and I are both therapists with a passion for helping individuals understand their attachment issues. We often delve into deep conversations about God, theology, psychology, and life's issues. We philosophize about a lot of things including the challenges that life throws at us. A few times I brought up the topic or thought that life is filled with loss.

Shannon said to me that he believes life is filled with loss. I believe that if an individual has lived life long enough and has taken risks that individual is going to endure loss. If an individual plays it safe and does not take risks, that individual may believe that he has no losses in his life. But he might be smart enough to understand that playing it safe creates its own losses.

The point is no one escapes loss in their life. Loss is a significant part of everyone's life. Most Americans want to believe that they have total control over their lives. Some fight for control with their spouses, with their bosses, with their college professors. The list goes on and so does the arguments for control. Many individuals are fear based.

These individuals attempt to be in control through avoiding their fears and often avoiding anything unfamiliar. I know people who have never traveled, who have never visited a national park or a new city. I know people who make all kinds of judgments about things that they have never experienced. It could be camping, hiking, skiing, traveling alone, going to college, or other things never ventured.

Other individuals have one bad experience, like flying, and they promise to never do it again. Stop and think what they might be missing out on. There are individuals who create an entire lifestyle based on fear. They have not given much thought to the philosophy, nothing ventured nothing gained.

If any individual were to really examine his or her life, he or she would discover that everything in life requires risk. Life contains no warranties. Warranties are for things, which usually break after the warranty has expired. There are risks that are not beneficial, like taking risks that place your life in physical danger. However, no one knows the outcome. There are no warranties in life.

When we can live life and make decisions with the philosophy that there are no warranties; we can begin to recognize our fears and let go of control. We can begin to understand ourselves and our reasons for the decisions we make. Every decision in life will be made with insufficient information. We will never have all the information that we would like to have in making a decision.

None of us have crystal balls to see the future. We feel strongly about certain things at particular points in our lives and we fall into a trap of believing that we always feel and think what we are feeling and thinking at the current moment in time.

In spite that we often base our decisions on our emotions; emotions are fleeting. This adds to the complexity of decision making. We often do not think things through. Even with big decisions, we don't think things through. We marry based upon our feelings of love toward the other person as well as how the other person makes us feel. We fall in-love and decide to marry without thinking about whether the person we love will be a good partner for us. More than fifty percent of marriages end in divorce. Another forty-five percent struggle to survive. So, approximately five percent of all marriages are happy marriages. We enter into jobs, sometimes careers based upon the present opportunity.

Often, we struggle because one decision in one direction leads to loss in another direction. We have to lose something to gain something else. This is a major component in the mental state of ambivalence. In order to accept a job position, we must lose a certain degree of freedom. With a job, we gain an occupation and money, but we lose freedom to do what we want during the course of the hours we are occupied at work.

For the past few decades, Americans have been attempting to buy into the philosophy that we can have it all. We can work, go to school, be involved in extra curricula activities, be involved in a relationship, raise children, and on and on. In recent years, we have been discovering and enduring burn-out, imbalance in our lives, and imbalance in our bodies and minds.

Something always suffers when we attempt to have it all. We cannot dedicate the same amount of energy to all of the activities in our lives. We must prioritize if we are going to have some degree of positive physical and mental health. If we don't let go of certain things, those activities will cause us health problems of some sort. Automatically, there is loss for something else that we are attempting to gain.

Americans have grave difficulty with this concept of gain and loss. A matter of fact, Americans are immature in our thinking that we can hold onto it all and still acquire more. We don't like to give up our activities, our things, our freedom, or any part of our lives. We believe we can multitask and that we have the time and energy to do everything we can possibly want to do.

Yet, if we were to evaluate our lives; we would find out that even with all the time saving devices in our lives and all the technological advances we have at our fingertips, we have no time and are more tired than individuals at our age than individuals at our age in past generations. We suffer because we want to hang onto it all and still want more.

We have grave difficulty understanding and accepting that it is natural to have to release certain activities in order to have other activities. We cannot be in more than one place at a given time. Most of us do not have the talent and ability to do everything well. Most of us have time constraints and other limitations. We struggle with what it is we want in life. We definitely struggle with giving up certain activities and certain relationships in order to gain new activities and acquire new relationships.

We have difficulty letting go. It is like having our hands full and attempting to grab for more. We do not value the concept of letting go. Yet, we are faced with the inevitable, which is our lives are constantly changing. There is loss all around us. Starting in our childhood, there is loss for every developmental stage. The Western world wants to focus on moving onto the next step forward. We don't take into full consideration the losses we have endured or are undergoing.

It is basically denying this significant part of our lives, loss. For every change there is loss. And it is in the manner that we deal with our losses that help us grow emotionally and spiritually. We have a choice to deny the reality of the losses in our lives, to go through life oblivious, to go through life not allowing ourselves to feel our emotions, or we can learn to grieve our losses and peacefully move forward.

We move peacefully forward we have achieved the final stage of grief, acceptance. The challenge is to be willing to acknowledge our losses and then to grieve them. Many individuals do not take the time to really savor the moment.

And most individuals really do not want to evaluate their past, even their most recent last chapter. It is more common to quickly move into our next chapter of our lives and act as if we have started at the present moment. In other words, we act as if the past is not significant.

The past helps shape our future. It is our past that influences the decisions we make in the present moment. It is the decisions we make in the present moment that begins to create the path we choose in the future. It is true that some individuals live their lives being emotionally stuck in the past. These individuals blame everyone and everything on their past and how they were treated. Then there are some individuals who are constantly fantasizing about their future. The goal is to live in the present.

But in order to live in the present, we must understand how we arrived at the place where we are. In order to understand how we arrived at this present place, we must acknowledge how our past helped influence our present moment. Part of that understanding must include being grateful for our past circumstances and the people that were there. Another part of that understanding must include grieving the past.

Why should we grieve the past? We need to grieve the past because otherwise, we carry it with us like unnecessary luggage. Grieving the past does not mean forgetting the past. It doesn't mean condoning the actions of people that have hurt us. Rather, it means being able to put the past to the past peacefully, recognizing the lessons we have learned, and acknowledging the fond memories.

One of my favorite lines in the movie, Forest Gump, was when Forest went running for three years back and forth across the country and Forest says, my momma always said you have to put the past behind you in order to move forward. Americans are in a hurry. We want to go into denial about the past or we want to carry it forward.

Neither works. We need to grieve

We need to recognize the loss we have experienced. We need to recognize how the past has influenced us and given us a stepping-stone into the future. We also need to be willing to say goodbye to the things that will never be again. An individual with a healthy secure internal working model can do this well.

The individual with a healthy secure internal working model recognizes his or her losses as a combination of those things that will never be again, and he/she recognizes how the past has influenced his or her presence and future. We will only be children once. When we are children doing cartwheels, riding a bike, playing outside all have special meaning. These are just some of the things that will never be again.

We only go through elementary school once in our lives. We can look back at our school days with fond memories. Some individuals will look back at their school days with emotional pain. Others will see their past elementary school days as a combination of both good and bad.

School is a perfect example of events in our lives that cannot be relived as well as events that have influenced our present and future. We must recognize our losses and grieve. We must also recognize our blessings and recognize how those decisions of our parents, teachers, and ourselves have influenced our present and future events.

Individuals, who have healthy secure internal working models, can grieve their losses, say goodbye to the things, events, and people of the past. These individuals who have healthy secure internal working models are also able to express gratitude for the people, things, and events that have influenced their presence and future events.

Individuals who have insecure and mis-wired internal working models struggle in several ways with their past. Some individuals with mis-wired internal working models have grave difficulty with letting go of their past and do everything to keep reliving it. Sometimes, this individual who can't seem to move forward stays emotionally stuck in his or her past, which can manifest into depression or anxiety.

Other individuals who get emotionally stuck in his or her past gets involved heavily into alcohol or drugs, in an attempt to forget about his or her past. Instead, he or she is in a vicious cycle of re-experiencing his or her emotional pain and using alcohol or drugs to mask the hurt.

Other individuals who have mis-wired internal working models believe that denial is a solution and he or she attempts to move into his or her future by stepping around or attempting to jump over his or her past. These individuals refuses to discuss his or her past. He or she also works hard at believing that all that counts is the present.

However, I find this individual in therapy for relationship issues and sometimes poor parenting. The reason why this individual is in therapy for poor parenting is that he or she have failed at recognizing that the mistakes that were done onto us that we just won't address creep out and get played out in their present moments and their future. We do often play out our childhoods in our adult lives by projecting our unfinished childhood wounds onto our adult partners, which causes poor adult relationships and often poor parenting as well.

7

Healing Our Wounds/Rewiring Our Internal Working Model

A significant part of healing and preventing poor adult relationships is healing from our past wounds. Many individuals will attempt to avoid facing their past believing that their past has no bearing on the present moment. Take a moment to think this through logically and you will soon discover this makes no sense. The reason we can or cannot do calculus is directly related to our success or failure in algebra. Our internal working model is created during our first six years of life.

It is during these first six years of life that we are supposed to master the concept of trust, learn about our emotions, and understand how to form a connection with another individual. It is also during these formative years that our logic for human connection is formed. It is during these formative years where we acquire the skills of recognizing our emotional needs, our physiological needs (food, shelter, safety), and cognitive needs and having each of our needs fulfilled.

Academic success at 16 years of age and older can be predicted at age two. Our relationship patterns pertaining to the characteristics we will seek out in an adult partner can be predicted in the formative years. And, even our sense of self-esteem and level of success can be predicted during these formative years.

The reason why we can make all these predictions is because our internal working model becomes wired during the formative years. Secondly, our internal working model is the executor for all aspects of our life, ranging from our relationships, our level of education, our self-esteem, and our level of success in life. When our internal working models become mis-wired due to our childhood wounds, we carry these wounds with us into and through our adult lives. We operate out of our mis-wired internal working model.

All of us have no choice but to view the world through our lens. Our lens comes from our experiences and our interpretations of the things that have happened to us, our interpretations of ourselves, others, and life itself. All of us view life and the things in which we experience differently from one another. Our experiences, our level of intelligence, our degree of sensitivity, and our perceptions all play a significant role along with our internal working model in our emotions, thoughts, and our behavior.

A very small percentage of the population has secure attachment, a securely wired internal working model. In the previous paragraphs, I described how all the different aspects of our life are connected to our internal working model. Another way to interpret the internal working model is to compare the internal working model to an invisible emotional and cognitive safety net. All of us need some type of security blanket, just like Linus (Charlie Brown's friend0.

Our internal working model is our emotional and cognitive security blanket. The internal working model executes our sense of security to take healthy risks in life. It is where our self-esteem is rooted so that we can actually feel a sense that we will be okay, whether we succeed or fail at a particular task or event. It is what exccutes our confidence that it is okay if we experience embarrassment, failure, success, rejection, etc. It is our internal working model that distinguishes our self-identity from our behavior, from our emotions, and from our thoughts.

The challenge for the majority of us is having a mis-wired internal working model. Therefore, our self-esteem, sense of confidence, and other aspects of our lives are negatively affected. In addition to a mis-wired internal working model, the majority of us grow up with negative childhood experiences. Negative internal messages are manifested out of our negative childhood experiences.

The process of how our internal messages get wired in our brains starts in childhood. As children we have an innate need to make sense out of the world in which we live in. Even infants have basic logic. Erik Erikson, in his eight stages of development throughout the lifespan, stated that infants acquire trust or mistrust through their own logic and memory of having their basic needs met.

In addition, children are egocentric, meaning that young children (under age 7) strongly believe that their thoughts come true. Young children also believe that what happens near them or around them is about them. They believe that they are the driving force behind all behavior, even when that behavior is from someone else.

So, children attempt to make sense out of their world, utilizing their logic. There are two significant challenges: 1) a child's world is pretty small, usually consisting of only immediate family members, and 2) children are utilizing logic at their level. As I stated earlier, the child interprets what is being done to them is their fault. This applies to child maltreatment as well.

Children interpret maltreatment toward them as their fault. One of the reasons for this is that it is not safe for the child to interpret their parents' behavior as good even when their parents' behavior is bad and hurtful toward the child. If the child views the parent as being bad, then the child's sense of security is basically completely gone. It is safer for the child to view themselves as bad and that their parent is acting according to the characteristics of the child.

So this is when we manifest and create our internal messages from our interpretations of the events, including traumas in our lives. In the diagram below, which I created to teach individuals how to disengage from power struggles and diminish their hurt. So, first, we will discuss triggers. Triggers are words, phrases, actions or a lack of actions from others that causes us to feel hurt, angry, sad, afraid, or causes us to be off kilter.

The next step is to understand the difference between how children think and the potential for how adults can think. Children have no choice but to believe that anything that happens near them or around them is about them. In addition, children have no choice but to personalize things. When children are bullied or picked on, they interpret that behavior as something wrong with them. Therefore, the pain from being bullied or called names is deep within a child. When the child is called names or criticized by their parents, the pain is enhanced exponentially.

Earlier, I discussed how our internal messages are the foundation for our executing functioning pertaining to our self-esteem, our interpretations of life around us, our confidence, and essentially our foundation for all aspects of our lives. So, we need to understand how our internal messages become wired.

Children need to understand the world in which they live in, in order for them to know if they are safe, who they can depend on, and how to survive. Children use their logic at the time of their traumas, and other vital events in their lives in their process of making sense of their world, including their traumas. Since, they are using their logic, they are most likely to determine that they are responsible for everything that has occurred in their life, including their traumas. In addition, children form the interpretation that if bad things happen to them, it because they are bad.

Children also commonly form the belief that they are their abuse. What happens to them is not only about them; it is happening because they are bad and deserve for it to happen to them. Children also form the belief that their identity is based upon how they are treated.

Since these beliefs and interpretations are formed in childhood. They are also filed away in our childhoods. Our interpretations and beliefs are wired into our internal working models. The younger we are when we experience trauma, the more impactful a mis-wired internal working model becomes.

Then, as adults, we operate automatically out of our mis-wired internal working models. One way this works is that our adult interpretations of what we hear or experience a behavior that comes out of our belief that we formed as a child. For example, when someone criticizes us in adulthood, it can easily stir up the pain we felt when we were picked on in our childhood. This is where our insecurities and defenses are rooted in. The majority of adults operate out of their childhood messages. Unfortunately, most adults interact with others, including their spouses, out of their mis-wired internal working models formed and wired in their childhoods.

As you can see in the diagram below, it is our internal messages that form our emotions. What we think is that someone says something or does something, and it is this individual's words or actions toward us that causes our emotions. Children have no choice but to think this way. What really occurs in the adult's brain is that someone says something to us or does something and we interpret the words or the actions according to our level of insecurities and our internal messages.

It is very similar to Piaget's concept of schemas. When someone calls us stupid, we feel angry and hurt. That anger and hurt is manifested from a history of low self-esteem combined with a history of feeling stupid or being called stupid. In contrast, if someone were to call you stupid and you have a history of good self-esteem and recognition for your intelligence, you won't feel as angry or as hurt because it is much easier for to recognize the speaker is the individual with the issue, not you. As you can also see on this road map (John's Trigger Wound Exercise), our internal messages drive our emotions, our self-esteem, our behaviors, and our thinking.

All of our psychological traumas are linked to our internal messages. As I stated earlier, our internal messages are manifested from our experiences, including our traumas. Our internal messages then become wired into our internal working model. Since our internal messages are wired into our internal working model, our internal messages drive our self-esteem, along with all other aspects of our executor functioning part of our brain.

How we present ourselves to how well we perform at our daily activities. Our academic success is manifested from our internal working model. Our level of functioning is most definitely wired in our internal working model. Our self-esteem and internal beliefs of ourselves are also wired in our internal working model.

I also believe that much of our mental wellness or lack of mental wellness comes from our internal working model. I firmly believe and know that both anxiety and depression are thinking disorders rather than genetic or biochemical disorders. Another way to view this is that our internal working model, most likely a mis-wired internal working model is responsible for our anxiety or depression.

The language which we use to describe ourselves as well as the language we use to describe the world in which we live in expresses our inner most thoughts about ourselves and the world which we live in. Our language is connected to our thoughts. Our thoughts are connected to our emotions. Both our thoughts and our emotions comprise our mind-set. It is our mind-set that creates a successful, confident life or a life filled with strife and overwhelming challenges.

Over thirty years of experience as a clinician has taught me that individuals who suffer from depression think differently, talk differently, and act differently than other individuals. I have found that individuals who struggle with depression think a lot. The depressed individual lives in his or her head. It is almost as if this individual has closed off the rest of his or her body and lives as if the only part of their body that is important is their brain and mind. This is in spite that their body may ache due to their depression.

In addition to living out of their brains and minds, these individuals think strictly negative thoughts. The depressed individual sees everything through a dark lens. Everywhere they look is something negative and appear blind to anything positive. In addition, the depressed individual often creates a downward spiral.

The downward spiral starts with only one negative thought that quickly creates five or six other negative thoughts. Each thought becoming more negative than the previous negative thought. Picture entering into a cave or a deep forest. In the beginning you can still see some light; however, as you walk further, the darker the area becomes. The same is true with a mental downward spiral. Thoughts become darker and our minds become heavier. Before we realize it, we are living in a dark place and attempting to evaluate and interact through a lens of darkness and depression.

Johns Trigger-Wound Exercise

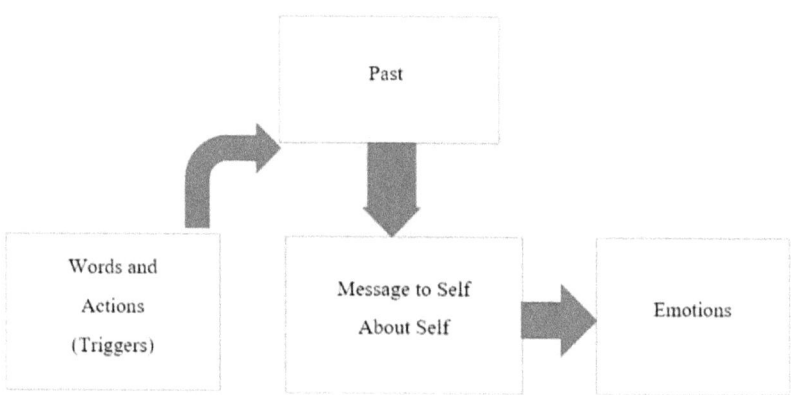

Anxiety is another thinking disorder. Those of us who struggle with anxiety live a lot of our lives in our minds and brains. Those of us who struggle with anxiety spend the majority of our days in our thoughts. We are always analyzing if things will work out the way we want, if we will survive, essentially, if we will be okay. A significant part of our analysis that involves all of the above questions also consists of writing movies in our minds that often involve tragedy, doom, heartache, or some emotional disaster. The good news is that almost every single time;

the real outcome is nowhere close to the disastrous outcome in our anxiety.

As I have been saying, our thoughts are powerful. When we change our thoughts, our emotions often change. When we change our thoughts, we behave differently. And, when we change our thoughts, our beliefs often change. Previously, I stated that it is our internal working model that executes our thoughts, beliefs, our emotions, and our behaviors. Well, a significant way to heal ourselves is to become aware of our thinking and to convert our thinking from negative to positive thinking. We learn through our thoughts how to be happier, behave better, and live more successful lives.

I will now discuss two major exercises to help convert negative thinking to positive thinking. First, it is imperative to always see the positives in ourselves. A great way to see the positives is to write about them. Create a positive journal. This is where you buy a notebook or journal, within your budget, and dedicate it toward writing only positive self-affirmations. Whether you believe it or not, keep adding at least one daily self-affirmation. Examine yourself through a positive lens. This is not about creating or building narcissism. Rather, this is about recognizing one's goodness. This is about recognizing that there is good in all of us. It is about being able to recognize what makes us. What are the positive qualities that you have that make up who you are?

Along, with building up positive traits, we need to diminish our negative thoughts. Think of a counter-balance scale or a teeter-totter with Positive thoughts sitting on one' side and negative thoughts sitting on the other side of the teeter totter. Whether it is the teeter totter or the counter balance scale, it is what weighs more in our life that will determine the outcome of our thinking. For example, when our positive thinking outweighs our negative thinking, we think more positive, behave positively and act happier. Eventually, we become happier,

As I just stated about the teeter totter and counterbalance scale, we need to diminish our negative thinking. The method that I came up with is very effective, efficient, and has demonstrated almost immediate positive results. Here is the method: you become in touch with your negative thoughts and negative beliefs about yourself. Sometimes, an individual will be aware of their beliefs about themselves, including their negative beliefs. So, this individual can write down beliefs like (I am not enough, I am stupid, I don't know anything, I can't do anything right, etc.).

Other individuals have difficulty knowing or being aware of their internal language. If these individuals are in touch with their emotions, then we can work on connecting emotions to thoughts. Then we can connect our thoughts to our internal language. For example, if someone tells us that we are stupid; sure, it is going to hurt a bit with a bit of shock. However, we are only going to react strongly because there is a part of us that believes it.

Remember, triggers are rooted in childhood, based upon our childhood traumas. So, if we were bullied in our childhood and called stupid, being called stupid as an adult is going to cause a much stronger reaction. One main reason is that we have created lies about ourselves, such as that we are stupid. We come up with all kinds of lies about ourselves when we have endured childhood abuse.

The reason for the lies is that the lies are an attempt to make sense of why we are being treated the way that we are being mistreated. It is an attempt to lessen the pain when we attempt to use the logic that we deserve to be mistreated. This is supposed less pain than to accept that the people who are supposed to love us the most actually do not love us at all.

The individual who has suffered much as a child, has many triggers and many issues. Childhood issues is where our insecurities come from. Childhood is where our internal messages are rooted. Utilizing my trigger-wound exercise is another way to get in touch with internal messages. Once you begin to list your internal messages, you can now evaluate your internal messages which form a theme. Some themes are: Respect, Not Being Good Enough, Feeling Inadequate, Rejection, and, Abandonment to name the more popular themes.

Our themes get wired into our internal working model. Our themes originate in our childhood based upon our childhood wounds and our interpretations of our childhood wounds and experiences. Then we live out of our beliefs including living out of our themes. We behave according to our beliefs about ourselves and our beliefs about the world in which we live in.

It is our beliefs, our internal messages, and our themes that give us our foundation for how we live our lives. This is where we learn our defenses, our coping mechanisms, and we behave according to those root themes in our lives.

Therefore, this is where depression is also rooted.

Depression is a thinking disorder. How we think about ourselves and how we think about the world in which we live in, determines our mood. As I stated earlier, when we think positive, we experience positive. When we think negative, we experience negative.

So, as I stated earlier, adding each day to your list of positive traits really enhances positive thinking and positive attitude. When you discard your negative thoughts, your negative beliefs, and your negative views of self and the world; you are left with thinking positive. The best method is to actually write out all your negative thoughts, negative labels, and negative beliefs on a sheet of paper. Then hand shred that paper continuously until there is nothing left to shred. As you hand shred these negative thoughts, say out loud "These are lies. These are lies. These are lies." And you keep saying that these are lies until there is nothing left to shred. Another component is to convert these lies into positive statements. Most of my clients state that they feel better almost immediately after this exercise. Our minds are powerful!

Another aspect of our powerful minds is our level of anxiety. Anxiety is also a thinking disorder. Individuals who struggle with anxiety often do a lot of thinking and it is usually negative thinking. A significant part of thinking while anxious involves dramatic and tragic endings. Essentially, individuals who struggle with anxiety write movies in their minds with tragic endings. Another significant component of anxiety is having difficulty that you will be okay.

I created a tripod of anxiety (shown below on next page) in order to express the three major components of how anxious individuals think and feel. All of us experience loneliness at times. However, most of us do not feel overwhelmed with feeling alone in the world. Individuals with anxiety feel alone in the world, especially when it comes to feeling anxious and solving the problem that is causing their anxiety. Individuals with anxiety also feel helpless.

The feeling that they are doomed and there is no solution to their problem creates a feeling of being helpless. In addition, individuals with anxiety also feel like they have no control. A feeling of helplessness vastly differs from a feeling of a lack of control. A feeling of a lack of control refers to feeling and believing that things are not in your control. The incident needs to be addressed in methods that are out of your control. While a sense of helplessness is more personal. A sense of helplessness is more related to feeling that there is something wrong with me, that I can't solve this problem.

Anxiety's Tripod

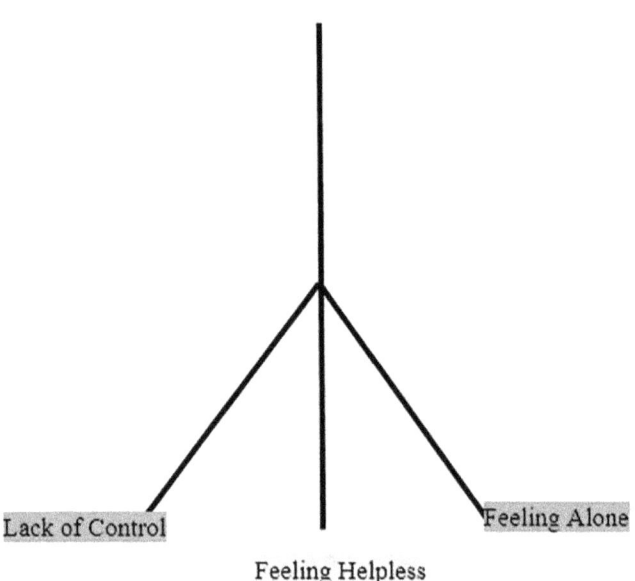

Utilizing the anxiety tripod, we can diminish our anxiety almost immediately as soon as we find something to do that is in our control. When we accomplish even the slightest thing toward solving our issue that is creating our anxiety. In addition, when we find that we have control, we often also feel less helpless.

In addition, utilizing logic is key when it comes to combatting anxiety. I created the cognitive processing flowchart shown on the next page. Since anxiety is a thinking disorder that usually involves irrational thoughts. When we think through our thoughts that are bringing us our anxiety, we often can work through our anxiety. We can determine that we are worried about things that we don't need to be worried about. If it is an issue that we do need to be concerned about, we can learn that we do have a solution to our problem. We will be okay.

When individuals have utilized the flowchart, they have found that they have the skills to work through their anxiety. They feel empowered. All of us feel in control and empowered when we take charge and do things within our control. The flowchart can be used for the majority of the situations or thoughts that are provoking anxiety. I highly suggest that individuals memorize the flowchart, in order to use when anxious in bed or anxious while driving or in a public place. By having the flowchart memorized, you can utilize it to work through many areas that provoke anxiety.

Cognitive Processing Flowchart

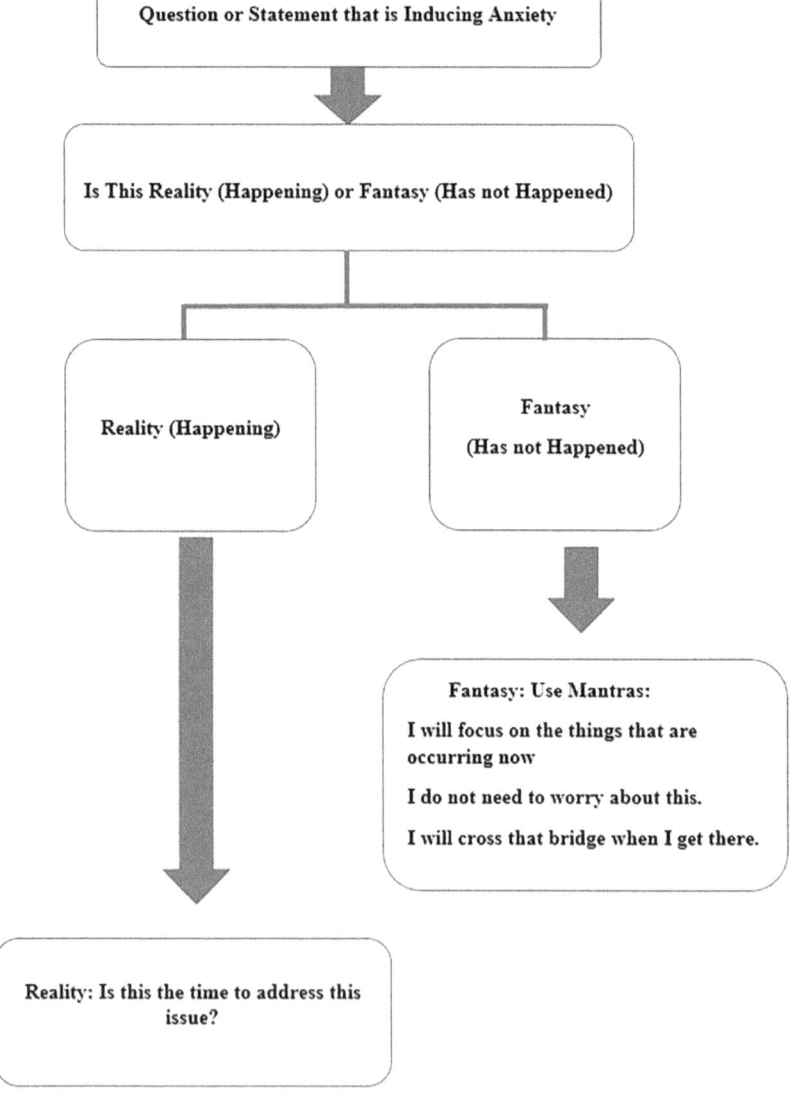

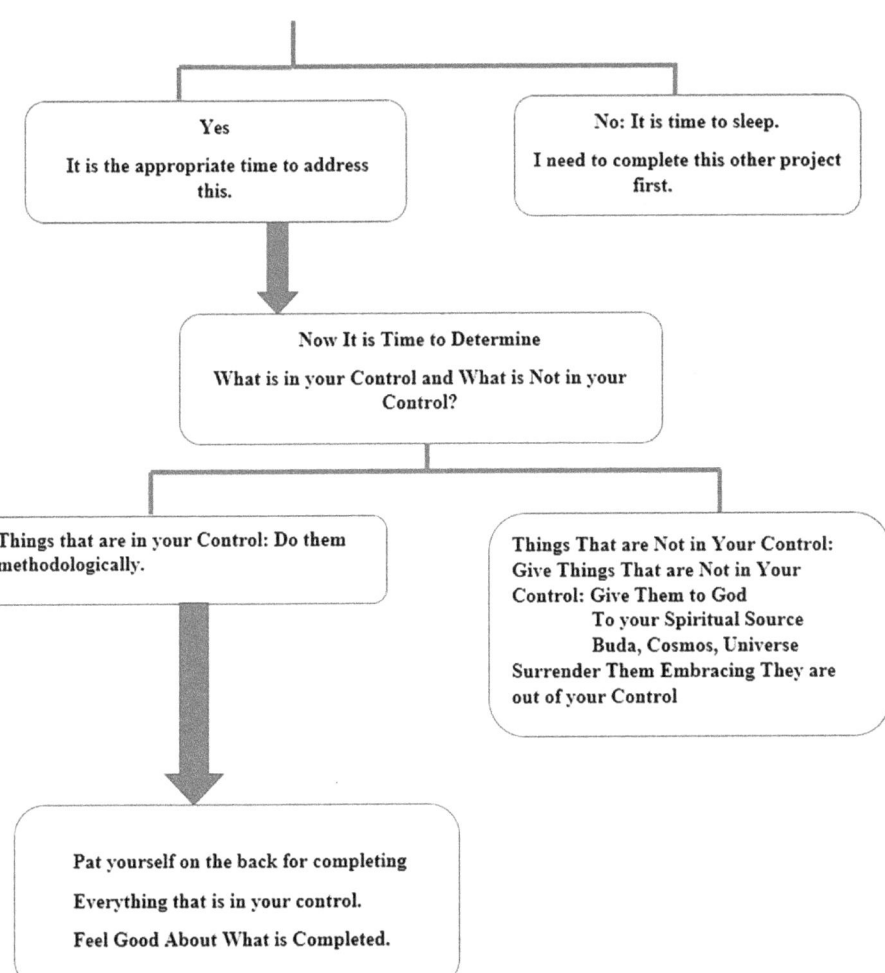

Another exercise to utilize with anxiety is called worst case scenario. This is where you actually play out the scenario as if you are a director in your own play. Then you evaluate the scenes pertaining to the likelihood of what you are imagining and often come to the conclusion that it is very unlikely that the event will play out as you imagine it to happen. The next evaluation is playing out worst case scenario and actually imagine living out the worst-case scenario. Now, you recognize that first, there is little chance of worst-case scenario occurring and even if it does, you will survive and be okay. This is empowering.

In addition to feeling empowered, we also need to feel relaxed, calm, and at peace. The best way to accomplish this is through a combination of the following three exercises. First, a daily walk of a thirty-minute, remembering this is not the time for any serious thinking, no serious discussions, and no problem-solving.

Working out kicks on our adrenalin and our central nervous system. Walking kicks on our parasympathetic system, which is responsible for calming. The second calming exercise is for four minutes at a time, take a sip of water, then take 5 deep breaths, then a sip of water then take 5 deep breaths. Do these alternations for four minutes at a time. Do this exercise three times a day. Over a period of ten days, individuals report that they have noticed their minds as quieter and being much calmer.

The third exercise is down time, which I have nicknamed dumbing time. All of us need to understand that in order to sleep, our minds need to be relaxed. In order for our minds to be relaxed, we need to actually practice shutting off our brains. So, the hour before we attempt to fall asleep, we practice shutting off our brains through not engaging in any serious discussion, not engaging in any conflicts, not paying bills, no watching the news, nothing serious or deep thinking. This is the time we need to shut off our brains and relax and calm ourselves. Then we are able to sleep.

The other areas that are involved in depression and anxiety is diet. First, it is extremely important to limit alcohol consumption and to limit any marijuana consumption. Fast food is also very bad, especially for both depression and anxiety. Sugar induces anxiety. Caffeine is also responsible for increasing anxiety. Energy drinks should not be legal, for energy drinks are poisonous to the brain, especially in the areas of depression and anxiety.

When we address all aspects of ourselves, the cognitive side, the emotional side, the physical side (diet and exercise), and our spiritual sides; we become healed and whole in positive ways. All aspects of ourselves affect our mental wellness.

When our mental wellness is deeply affected due to an extensive history of childhood maltreatment (abuse or neglect), we can heal through some heavy therapy of reparenting. Re-parenting has a major goal of healing those deep childhood traumas and the effects of those traumas. In addition to working on internal messages and beliefs about self, in this therapy, we are going to work toward nurturance and self-love.

The most powerful method of working toward nurturance and self-love is to live it daily. When clients are ready to do this heavy work, I have them start by going out and purchasing a stuffed animal that represents themselves. Then, since language and touch together have been shown to strongly imprint messages into the brain, we are going to utilize this method to rewire our mis-wired internal working model.

The first step is for you to purchase a stuffed animal that represents yourself. The stuffed animal does not need to be expensive, it does not matter the size. What matters is the resemblance of self. The next part of this long therapeutic exercise/method is to recognize and acknowledge the characteristics that are in common between the stuffed animal and self. At this point, it is also very imperative to name the stuffed animal. This is a projective therapeutic exercise. A projective exercise is an exercise that basically personifies the stuffed animal.

Since, you are personifying the stuffed animal. I teach clients to greet their new friend each and every day. I also teach that each time you say goodbye, whether it is to go to work or to go out, you take a moment to explain that you are going out but is coming back. This short vignette helps significantly to heal any abandonment issues, as long as it is done on a consistent basis. Then at the end of the evening, I have clients form an additional habit of saying good night to their stuffed animal. In addition, you will create other times for dialog with your new special friend.

It is through this combination of touch and language, that you are having your internal working model rewired. This projective exercise shows its power every day through the internal connections of self-love, nurturance, cognitive, and emotional connections. When individuals take the time and the diligence to work this exercise daily, there is a lot of deep healing that takes place.

This exercise is also attachment therapy. That is how your internal working model becomes rewired. Through the combination of getting rid of negative internal messages, increasing our positive internal messages, changing our emotions to positive and happier, and doing attachment therapy with our stuffed animals, will achieve rewiring our internal working models.

This takes time, diligence, steady work of facing our wounds and working through our traumas. We need to recognize how our wounds and traumas have affected us in our relationships, academics, work, and all other aspects of our lives. Then, we need to be willing to work diligently on changing our internal messages in order to change our emotions and then change our behaviors. Finally, we need to work hard to strive to live out of a healthy attitude and strive toward our pursuit of happiness. We are reliving our lives, but this time with happiness, passion, and purpose.

8

Becoming Proactive with Our Children

In addition to healing our childhood wounds, we need to learn to do things differently than how we were parented. We graduate from parenting at the age of six. In other words, we automatically parent the way in which we were parented. The way in which we were parented is wired into our internal working model. We have been discussing our internal working model throughout this book.

In spite that we most likely do not have distinct memories of our entire first six years, we have these memories stored in our bodies (through our cell membranes). We also have our autonomic memories stored in our internal working models. Remember, I discussed earlier that our internal working models execute our thoughts, emotions, attitudes, and behaviors.

However, we are not robots. Therefore, when we become self-aware, we are free to re-wire our internal working models. One way we to become very self-aware is through gaining education in our parenting and parenting philosophy. Through mindfulness, we can become very mindful (conscientious) parents and conduct conscientious parenting.

A significant act of mindful parenting is holding a child. For centuries, mothers have been holding their babies to their chest. Sometimes, mothers do this to breastfeed their child. Other times, mothers hold their babies basically to carry their babies to get done what they need to get done. And there are times when mothers just hold their babies to their chests for their babies to sleep there. However, it has not been automatic to think about the relationship between mother's breast and her heart to their baby.

Attachment begins in the womb listening to mother's heart. From conception, there is a living being with a relationship to their mother. I discussed the majority of this in chapter three. The one thing I will add here is that you cannot over hold a baby. Some parents are concerned that if you pick up a child every time, that you spoil a child.

If a parent were to pick up the child when the child is crying, when the child is having a temper tantrum, is happy, sad, is angry, etc. The child receives the message that they get picked up no matter what. They also receive the message that they are loved, taken care of, safe, and secure.

The research I conducted during my dissertation taught me that the most key component for a child's success is the parent's ability to parent with sensitivity toward the child's needs. It is not about spoiling the child; rather, it is about guiding, directing, and disciplining your children with sensitivity toward the child's needs. This creates a foundation of success for the child.

A significant component of the child's success is the parent wiring in their child's internal working model the ability to regulate their emotions. A significant component to mental health is emotional stability. A significant aspect of emotional stability is the ability to regulate our emotions. Emotions are fleeting. We seldom stay happy and calm for any extended period of time. Rather, we experience a wide range of emotions through a large number of diverse and complex interactions throughout any given day. It is our ability to regulate our emotions throughout the day in response to all of these multifaceted interactions that brings us peace and the ability to reconcile all of these interactions with peace and contentment.

The majority of individuals who struggle with being able to maintain peace and contentment in their lives come from childhoods filled with anxiety, anguish, lacking trust, and struggle with all types of insecurities. Our insecurities manifest our defense mechanisms, and both are rooted in our childhood wounds.

Stating the obvious, as parents we want to avoid causing harm to our children as much as possible. The challenge is multifaceted. First, the problem becomes more challenging the more a parent comes from a painful and challenging childhood. We parent the way in which we were parented. During the first six years of life, while our internal working models are being wired, we are acquiring our parenting skills, which are also becoming wired in our internal working model.

We parent the way in which parenting comes natural to us. What comes natural is how we were treated as children. We also learn about our emotional regulation during these formative years. In addition, we learn how to feel about ourselves, treat ourselves as well as how to treat others. As I stated earlier, our internal working models function as our major executor for the majority of our cognitive and emotional components.

When our internal wiring models are wired by parents who have mis-wired internal working models, our internal working models become mis-wired. Attachment is intergenerational. This is how childhood maltreatment, such as abuse and neglect become intergenerational. We parent and often treat our children in the manner in which we were treated as children.

The best gift any parent can give to their child is a healthy parent. A healthy parent is the parent who attends parenting classes on a regular basis. A healthy parent is also the parent who attends therapy in order to bring healing to their childhood wounds and makes a very mindful (conscientious) decision to parent differently than how they were parented.

The ideal parent also utilizes the child's sensitivity to meet the child's needs. Attunement, the parent's ability to read, know, and understand the child's physical, cognitive, and emotional needs is highest when the parent is sensitive to the child's needs. Attunement is an imperative component to attachment. In addition, they practice on a daily basis to parent in healthy ways that are most beneficial to their children.

As I have been discussing throughout this book, creating a healthy secure attachment with a positively wired internal working model is the ultimate goal. I dedicated the previous chapter to several methods of healing from our childhood wounds. I will say this again, "The greatest and most valuable gift any parent of any socioeconomic background can give to their children is a healthy parent. The second greatest gift any parent can give to their children is a securely wired internal working model.

In addition to holding your baby, meeting your children's emotional needs, cognitive needs, and physical needs, you are inducing trust and a secure internal working mpdel through your emotional, physical, and cognitive consistency. It is vital to a child's mental wellness as well as an adult's mental wellness to be able to trust others, depend upon others, and be consistent with their words, emotions, and actions. When parents provide this type of consistency for their children, they are enhancing their child's mental wellness and their child's secure internal working model.

Attachment theory also states that the environment for the child creates patterns within the brain that tells us our identity (who we are), the way in which we interpret our environment in reference to ourselves, and the bond which we formed or did not form with our parents. It is in this mental blueprint, which is formed from our parent-child relationship, that we learn how to react to the world and how to interact with others.

It is through the hundreds of thousands of our parent-child interactions that we learn about trust, dependability, predictability, and our self-worth. Trust is earned over time through consistency in behaviors (Stephen Arterburn). An individual can also exhibit untrustworthiness. It is through their consistent behavior that will determine whether to trust or not. When our parents use consistent behaviors that earn trust within the child, then a healthy secure internal working model is formed. When our parents use consistent behaviors that do not earn trust, then a mis-wired internal working model is created.

In order to enhance the parent-child relationship and to enhance secure internal working models (secure attachment), I designed a technique I call Gentle Connections. Gentle Connections is where a parent holds her/his child close to their chest and makes sure the child hears his/her heartbeat. In order to make sure the child is actually hearing your heartbeat, take your child's hand and tap out two different rhythms.

The rhythms do not have to be scientific or perfect musical rhythms. They just need to be different rhythms. This will entice the child to maneuver their head to actually hear their parent's heartbeat. Then the parent counts out loud and slowly to 30. So this lasts at least a full minute. The ultimate best times to do gentle connections is right before the child goes to bed and then in the morning as the child begins their day.

Another attachment technique is for the parent to consistently tell their child that mommy or daddy is in your heart. So as a parent, ask your child, when mommy is at work or you are in school, where is mommy? And the ultimate answer is mommy is in my heart. This technique enhances attachment and a securely wired internal working model.

A securely attached child is on their way to a health productive, happy successful life. Attachment is the foundation of life, of all pathology, of our sense of security, and our behavior. When we enhance the attachment within our children, we also enhance their sense of security and their self-esteem. When we enhance our children's sense of security and their self-esteem, we also diminish their misbehavior.

All of us behave according to our beliefs about ourselves and others. Parents have a lot of power in creating an individual who will be a lover of people or an individual who will be a criminal. When parents heal their childhood wounds, they are giving the greatest gift of all, a healthy secure parent with a securely attached internal working model. It takes a healthy parent to raise a securely attached child.

Another significant component to raising a securely attached child is for the parent to set limits and boundaries with their children that exemplify the values and beliefs they would like their children to embrace. During four decades of teaching parent education, I would say that parents struggle the most with setting limits and boundaries for their children.

I have also found that there are several reasons why parents struggle with this concept of setting limits for their children. The largest percentage of parents in the \United States, in the past several decades, are single parents. Single parents have the stress and challenge of working all day, getting home and cooking, cleaning, and getting their children ready for bed and their next day. In addition, a single parent who is divorced often feels the need to compete with their ex (co-parent) for their child's affections and really does not feel confident in risking their relationship with their child.

The combination of limited time and the belief that the parent will risk their child's love leads to parents either only reacting emotionally and either not setting limits or not following through with setting limits. The challenge with ideal and ultimate parenting is that it does take time to set this up for you and your child in a positive and non-reactionary manner.

However, if you want the ultimate best for your child, then the parenting has to be the ultimate best. The ultimate best parenting, as stated earlier, is a healthy you. A healthy you is going to get talking with your ex about the values and traits you both want to instill in your child.

It is from the values and traits that you want to instill in your child that the rules are derived from. The rules you set for your children combined with following through with the discipline you engage with your children will exemplify the values and traits you want to instill in your children. If it is important to you that your child speaks respectfully and you make that a rule for your child and discipline your child with the goal of speaking respectfully, then you and others will experience your child as speaking respectfully. If it does not matter to you of how your child speaks to others, then it will show through how your child speaks disrespectfully to others.

So, the first step is for each parent to come to an agreement on the values and traits you want to instill in your children. The next step is to derive a set of rules for your children that will exemplify your family values and the traits you want to instill in your children.

The next step is for the two parents to agree upon the rules and agree upon the consequences. One of the challenges parents have is not following through with setting consequences for their children. Some parents are actually afraid that setting consequences with their children will disturb their relationship with their children. Other parents don't want to do the work involved with setting boundaries with their children. Other parents become emotionally reactive when their children misbehave.

The biggest challenge in parenting is the emotions that are involved. As humans, it is very easy to personalize another person's behavior especially if the behavior is from someone we love and the behavior is happening around us or toward us. It is a process to accept that another person's behavior even directed toward you is not about you. We simply do not have control over another individual nor their behavior. All of us are born with free will.

Free-will allows us to choose how we want to emotionally react or respond to another individual's behavior, including their words. Therefore, another individual can only really be discussing their reaction to their experience of us. But they can only speak of their experience of us. They do not have the ability to determine what we are thinking or what we are feeling. They can insult us, attack us either emotionally, verbally, or physically; but they have no ability to know our thoughts nor our emotions. This applies to both adults and children.

So, by having set limits and consequences for our children takes the emotions out of the equation when it comes to disciplining. The rules have been agreed upon between both parents and they have been stated and explained to your children. The best way to explain rules and consequences to young children (less than age 10) is by creating an individualized incentive chart for each of your children.

An incentive chart is a picture of how rules, rewards, and consequences will be for your child. A good incentive chart is very simple; one axis lists the days of the week and the other axis lists the behaviors (being in bed on time, being ready for school on time, no trouble in school, no bad words, completing homework, completing a chore).

When your child completes one of these tasks/behaviors for the day they receive a point. When your child does not complete a particular task, they receive nothing. Incentive charts are based upon strictly positive reinforcement. A child can only receive a reward for his or her completion of tasks.

Therefore, it is significant that the two parents actually determine what is the least amount that the child needs to do in order to receive the lowest reward. For example, if there are ten tasks, the recommended maximum number of activities listed on an incentive chart, a third of ten is approximately three points. Three successful activities completed multiplied by seven days equals twenty-one.

So, the minimum number of points your child must earn to receive a reward is twenty-one points. So, your child chooses a reward that you and your child have previously agreed upon that would fit this category. Then you have a medium reward of 22 to 55 points and your child would receive a medium reward, again that you have previously agreed upon. Fifty-six points to 70 points earns the ultimate high reward that you and your child agreed upon before you started using the incentive chart. I have thousands of parents over thirty years state to me how well this works, how excited their child becomes when earning points and how much easier and less emotionally reactive the parent becomes.

Incentive charts are also the easiest way to stay on track as a parent and follow through. We discussed earlier how important the first year of life is, how important holding is, and how important it is to wire your child's internal working model as securely attached.

Well, the journey continues with setting limits and boundaries for your child. The second-year bonding cycle creates trust and security for your child through consistently setting limits and boundaries. At this stage, a child is forming a habit of constantly asking his or her parent for things as well as wondering where the boundaries lie. When a parent keeps their yes to a yes and their no to a no, then trust is formed. When a parent's yes turns to a no the child loses trust in his parent. When a parent changes their no to a yes; it may seem like the child has won and will be happy, but actually trust has been broken.

When your child becomes an adolescent, then it is time for you to convert incentive charts into written contracts. This is a similar process of discussing with your co-parent what is important to teach your children and what traits you want your adolescent child to start exhibiting.

Then, you determine what rules need to be instilled in order to teach those traits as well as in order to produce a healthy productive adult-child. You also want to be thinking about rules need to be enhanced in order to create structure, security, and love within the household and avoid chaos and apathy at all costs.

Your adolescent child also gets to participate by stating the items and privileges he would like to earn. Then the parent types the contract and each person signs it. Then there are several copies in order to prevent the times when your adolescent child decides to become a cocky teen who attempts to tell you that either he never received a contract or that it is lost and you present him with a new copy. Again, this is at the stage of one of the final steps of creating a securely attached internal working model.

Let's briefly discuss the consequences of parents not setting limits and boundaries with their children. Some parents are just lazy and prefer to not get stressed for any reason, including being involved in their children's lives. Other parents simply are not experienced in knowing that children need to have limits and boundaries. And, there are also parents who think that they are setting limits and boundaries with their children when they are telling their children to not do something. As I stated earlier, this has been found to be the most difficult challenge, besides following through, for parents.

So, what are the long-term consequences for children when parents do set limits and boundaries with their children? First, we need to understand that all individuals function much better when operating off of a schedule and create structure for ourselves. Children actually thrive from structure. Trust is earned over time through consistent behavior. Our observations can tell us who is dependable, who is caring, who is empathetic, and who is self-absorbed and not trustworthy.

Children thrive on structure because structure sets the stage for predictability, emotional safety, and security. All of us are cautious of taking risks, no matter how safe the risk may be, our self-esteem often will determine the amount of risk taking we will engage in. Yes, the more securely attached (securely wired internal working model), the higher our self-esteem.

However, our children's securely attached internal working model is partially due to the parent's ability and willingness to set limits and boundaries with their children. In addition, the process of limits and boundaries builds an internal structured infrastructure system, which is a significant part of our internal working model. A major component of our internal infrastructure system, which is manifested from the process of limits and boundaries, is our internal safety net. This safety net is manifested in our self-confidence to take risks. If something does not go right, we return to our safety-net and we are secure.

So what happens when limits and boundaries are not created and not set by the parent for the child? The child struggles in school. The child struggles academically because their brain is lacking structure, which is a necessary tool for mastering mathematics, writing and reading. In addition, children who lack having limits and boundaries set by their parents will have a continuous problem with misbehaving on a consistent and regular basis.

This is where oppositional defiance disorder comes in and conduct disorder begins to develop. Often, the individual who has struggled with not having structure and lacks limits and boundaries turn to either the military to learn limits and boundaries or this individual ends up in jail or homeless. Setting limits and boundaries for your children is a great gift that a parent can give to their children,

When limits and boundaries are set on a regular basis, the likelihood of engaging in power struggles with your children significantly diminish. Power struggles occur because there are two individuals who are struggling with their insecurities, along with struggling with the need for power and control.

When this occurs between a parent and their child, the parent is becoming more frustrated with themselves and their child. The child is unaware of what is really happening because they think they can get what they want; however, if the child wins the power struggle with their parent, they actually lose. It is not safe for a child to be in charge and have total control, just like it is not safe for passengers on a plane to have total control or to be in charge. When parents take charge and are in control, their child is both physically and emotionally safe. This safety creates the child's emotional safety net so the child can feel confident in taking healthy risks.

It is healthy and important for a child to take healthy risks, exploring their world, learning new things and discovering more each day of who they are. We don't know if we are going to enjoy something until we do it. There is only way to determine if we are going to enjoy something and that is by doing it. All of us have images in our minds of what we think something will be like. However, those images are based upon inadequate information. Exploration is a significant component of learning anything, including learning about ourselves.

Another significant parenting practice is allowing your child to explore within healthy parameters. A securely attached internal working model provides us a safety net and executes healthy risks from unhealthy risks. It is imperative for a parent to see their child objectively. This is a major challenging objective for any of us. We want to see the people we love in the way we want to see them. Love can blind us.

With raising children, not only does our love blind us; but also our hopes and dreams for our children can also get in the way. When we love someone, we want what we think is the best for them. We make these judgments and decisions based upon our experiences, both good and bad.

Sometimes, parents project upon their children, talents and wishes that their child really does not have. The parent who does this is attempting to live vicariously through their child the broken or incomplete dreams that the parent had as a child. This is very unfair to the child and can be considered emotionally abusive because the parent's job is support their child in assisting their child in fulfilling the child's dreams.

One of the things that often gets in the way is that parenting becomes very challenging when the child becomes the age the parent was when the parent experienced a significant trauma. This is what occurs: parenting is going well and there is a wonderful parent-child relationship, however, as the child grows and becomes the age the parent was when the parent experienced a significant trauma, the parent becomes extremely anxious and often reactionary.

Especially, if the parent's childhood trauma is unresolved, the parent is emotionally reactionary and often projects their trauma up on their child. Now there is an attachment break, creating a disconnection in what was once a wonderful parent-child relationship.

This disconnected parent-child relationship can be repaired. Self-Awareness is almost always the first step of healing any trauma and any issue. We have to know what we are repairing. We have to know what to address, knowing what the problem is.

The next step is for the parent to enter into therapy and heal from their childhood trauma. Part of that healing will encompass the parent learning that their child is a different person than they are living a different life than the parent and having a different parent than what the parent had. Then the parent can rebuild and enhance their relationship with their child.

The parent-child relationship is perhaps the most complex form of relationship as well as the most sensitive. The parents' internal attachment patterns, which is the bond that they formed or did not form with their parents significantly influences the child now and the development of the child into adulthood. As stated previously, all of us graduate from parenting school at age six and are prone to parent the way we were parented. It requires mindfulness and conscientious effort to parent differently. Other factors influencing the parent-child relationship involve resources, beliefs, and attitudes.

Life is not fair nor is it equal for everyone. Different individuals have different resources. Some individuals have family members to help them with their children. Some individuals are more educated than others and other individuals are more educated about parenting skills than other individuals.

Some individuals have the huge blessing of growing up in a loving and functional home with healthy parents. Other individuals grew up in horrendous environmental factors and abusive parents. We do not all have the same starting point. True success is how much you have transformed your situation and the things that were done onto you.

All of this influences your child in major significant ways. This is why I have mentioned several times that the greatest gift you can give to your child is a healthy you. Other significant factors is the ability to acquire and maintain a united front with your co-parent. Every child comes into this world with the same mission; that is to divide and conquer. When the child wins the challenge of divide and conquering their parents; the child actually loses.

We discussed earlier the importance of the parent being in charge and being in control for the benefit of the child. If the child wins control, the child loses their sense of safety, their sense of security and their confidence to explore and learn because their built-in safety net is not there.

There is a lot involved in the science of parenting. To do parenting correctly, it involves a lot of self-awareness of our actions as well as understanding why we do what we do and being aware of our attitudes toward our children as well as attitudes and beliefs about our child's education and the world in which the child lives in. It is well worth the money, the work, and the time invested in therapy to become the ultimate parent.

9

Understanding How Attachment is the Foundation of All Pathology

Psychopathology in the adolescent and adult years are rooted in the early years of our lives from our insecure and mis-wired internal working models. Social and emotional behavior in adulthood is correlated with the mental wellness of that individual in their first six years of life. Remember, insecure or secure attachment creates our internal working models. It is our internal working models that can be wired for secure-attachment or we can have a mis-wired internal working model that creates some type of insecure-attachment.

As I mentioned throughout this book, it is our internal working model that executes our self-esteem, the discernment to determine healthy risks from unhealthy risks, and our sense of confidence to problem solve and think things through. It is our attachment foundation that determines our willingness to acknowledge our emotions and our ability to empathize

As you have been learning, humans have a foundation. That foundation is called childhood. And the most imperative parts of our childhood are the foundational years (0-6) and the relationship that the parent creates with his or her children. Erik Erikson stated that the first year of life is when trust is formed and wired internally in us through the relationship with our parents. Trust occurs when the parent meets the needs of his or her child. Trust is earned over time through consistent behavior. Trust is either earned through the child consistently having his needs met or trust is not earned because the child cannot trust that his needs will be met.

The next stage of development after trust has been formed or not formed is another sense of security. In this sense of security, parents are supposed to be teaching as well as creating limits and boundaries with their children. It is during this stage of development that exemplifies the loudest later in life. When parents set limits and boundaries with their children, they are creating an internal safety net for their children. When children acquire a built-in safety net, the child learns to take healthy risks and learns to explore his or her environment.

Exploring one's environment is vital to one's educational and intellectual development. In addition, the child with an internal safety net has the wiring in their internal working model for creating structure and an executor that stays focused, maintains healthy boundaries, and develops the ability for success in academics as well as success in life. When parents do not set limits and boundaries with their children, the child lacks having a built-in safety net has grave difficulty with structure, learning, following rules, staying focused, and being successful.

Children who grow up without limits, grow up without structure, and have grave difficulty with authority and following rules. These children often grow into adults who are more prone to having difficulty holding down a job, acquiring success in school, and more likely to get in trouble with the law. Some of these individuals recognize the need to acquire a built-in safety net and therefore join the military, The military serves as mother telling an individual when to awake, what to wear, how to wear it, how to do each task with structure, methodically, and with care and pride.

A common theme throughout this book has been the significance of a healthy secure attachment and a healthy wired internal working model. In this chapter, I am discussing how attachment is the foundation for all pathology. Another significant component of pathology and trauma is the age of onset.

For example, the conscience is formed at the end of the first year of life, when a child's needs are met on a consistent basis. The conscience is responsible for telling us right from wrong. The conscience is also connected to an individual feeling a healthy shame and guilt when one offends. All of these thoughts and emotions do not become wired in an individual's internal working model, when attachment goes awry.

When a child's needs are not met on a consistent basis, the child's conscience is not formed. Now, since the child's conscience is not formed, then you have a sociopath individual. It is this simple! When people do the things that were designed by God to do, then wonderful things happen and when individuals conduct horrific acts then horrific things are manifested. Psychologists often refer to sociopath individuals as individuals who have antisocial personality disorder. The crux of the antisocial personality disorder is having no positive regard for another human being.

This individual without a conscience lives a life of not having any empathy and no positive regard toward another human being. In spite, that it is federal law that a child, defined as younger than 18 years of age, cannot be given the diagnosis of antisocial personality disorder. Antisocial personality disorder is the psychology diagnosis and term used interchangeably with sociopath.

Children who are young sociopaths are given the diagnosis of conduct disorder and oppositional defiant disorder instead of the diagnosis of antisocial personality disorder. A clinician who specializes in attachment therapy will diagnose a child with sociopathic tendencies as having reactive attachment disorder.

Again, sociopaths are not born; they are created. The majority of pathology is rooted in our childhood. |The majority of pathology is rooted in our mis-wired internal working models and our insecure attachment patterns. Everything in psychology is developmental, meaning it is manifested over time and circumstances. This includes the violent sociopath, who receives an adrenalin rush/induce after their actual act of violence. No one wakes one day and decides to kill another human being or to intentionally hurt someone. This is bred over time. The sociopath is created during the first year of life.

The sociopath as a young toddler associates the world as an unsafe and untrusting place, where they must meet their own needs. Then it develops into a young child who is very withdrawn and uncaring towards others. Then this individual with antisocial personality disorder might commit their first act of violence through a fight or an act of physically bullying another child.

Then this same individual might commit a deeper sense of violence and kill the family pet, even as an experiment of experiencing what it is like to kill something and what goes on for the other living thing to die. A great book on this topic is Children Without a Conscience by Ken Magid. The point is behaviors, personalities, beliefs, and attitudes are wired into our internal working models. When parents create positive experiences for their children, positive self-esteem and beliefs are wired. When parents do not create positive experiences for their children, then negative beliefs and low self-esteem are wired into the child's internal working model.

As I mentioned earlier, reactive attachment disorder is manifested from a miswiring of the child's internal working model. As I also mentioned earlier this mis-wired internal working model is manifested from severe pathological neglect during the child's first year of life. So, essentially sociopath, antisocial personality disorder, and reactive attachment disorder are all the same disorder. These terms are basically synonyms. Reactive attachment disorder is one of the four types of insecure attachment typologies.

Another insecure typology is called disorganized attachment disorder. This attachment pattern is a term designed by Mary Main in 1988. When Mary Main was conducting attachment research between mothers and their very young children, she noticed a strange phenomenon. Mothers went through all the right moves in order to calm their distressed child. In spite that the mothers engaged in all the right techniques that would ease a child's distress; this time the child stayed distressed as well as demonstrated fear toward their primary caregiver, their mother.

The characteristics include unresolved childhood wounds and trauma, insecure attachment with their parents, a significant degree of emotional insecurities, and very fearful patterns for connection. In other words, Main discovered that attachment patterns are intergenerational. A mother who has unresolved childhood wounds cannot create a healthy securely attached child without first healing their own childhood wounds.

Another significant factor that Main discovered was that attachment goes way deeper than just going through the correct steps. Attachment involves a very deep emotional, spiritual, and intuitive connection between mothers and children. The mother child connection is a very deeply sacred relationship. This is the ultimate most sacred relationship more than all other relationships put together.

Contemporary psychologists view the etiology (root cause) of disorganized attachment pattern as inconsistent parenting. Some psychologists have even noticed that there are parents who will add emotional abuse, such as making fun of their child for having an emotional hard time, or dismissing their child's emotions, or actually punishing their child for having emotions.

It is often seen in individuals who have been sexually abused, physically or verbally abused. These types of parenting patterns and behaviors will definitely create disorganized attachment patterns within their child. The child will become an adult with disorganized attachment style.

As adults, the internal working model of an individual who has disorganized attachment style can easily also have borderline personality disorder. Other manifestations of disorganized attachment style would include substance abuse or depression. There is also going to be a manifestation of a lot of ambivalence within the individual towards significant relationships. This individual wants to be in a relationship but does not trust and is waiting for rejection.

Since the root of disorganized organized attachment disorder is early childhood; therefore, children can have disorganized attachment disorder. The symptoms of disorganized attachment disorder in childhood include significant ambivalence showing the child loves his or her parents and even cares for them, but at the same time is afraid of their parents. In addition, a child with disorganized attachment disorder will set themselves up to be rejected by their peers and friends. This child will also sabotage their own success academically as well as in their behavior by getting into trouble for stupid things, stealing and then making it known that they are the person who is responsible for the theft. Most psychologists, including myself, believe that understanding and treating disorganized attachment style is the most complex attachment pattern.

The disorganized attachment style is becoming the fastest growing and most popular attachment style. In many ways, this makes a lot of sense within our culture. Generations spiral downward in numerous ways, including education, altruism, empathy, emotional maturity, and attachment patterns. Now can parents go to therapy, heal their wounds and acquire skills to raise healthier children than themselves and actually raise healthy children? Yes, we can do this mission and we should complete this mission of raising healthy children. But in the meantime, the disorganized attachment style is growing amongst the population.

Another type of insecure attachment disorder is the anxious/ambivalent attachment pattern. A contemporary name for this attachment pattern is preoccupied attachment style. Both terms are interchangeable. One of the reasons why I like the term preoccupied is because a lot is said in the term. An individual struggling with anxious-ambivalent attachment disorder is preoccupied with thoughts of wondering if he or she will be cheated on, taken advantage of, or hurt in some way.

The way that adults with anxious-ambivalent or preoccupied attachment disorder attempt to protect themselves from being hurt is by keeping emotionally distant, withdrawing at times, or not trusting that they are loved.

If you believe that you are not loved, you might also believe that you are not worthy of love and therefore, you understand why your partner would leave. Individuals with anxious-ambivalent attachment disorder also struggle with high anxiety about the relationship and connections in their lives. Some individuals who struggle with anxious ambivalent attachment disorder also struggle with social anxiety. Some individuals who struggle with anxious ambivalent attachment disorder can also manifest BPD (Borderline Personality Disorder). BPD is often associated with abandonment issues. Other adults struggling with anxious-ambivalent attachment disorder struggle with substance abuse as well.

All adult struggles are rooted in childhood. All attachment patterns become manifested in early childhood. As anxious-ambivalent attachment disorder is manifested in childhood; there are behaviors that children display anxious-ambivalent attachment disorder. The behaviors displayed by children include being weary of strangers, becoming greatly distressed when parents leave and yet not feeling comforted when parents return.

Another insecure attachment typology is the avoidant attachment pattern. Within the avoidant attachment typology lies several subsets or patterns such as the dismissive avoidant attachment pattern. Individuals who struggle with dismissive-avoidant attachment disorder are often secretive, rigid in their ideas and beliefs. In addition, this individual avoids relationships and either has casual and short-lived romantic relationships or no relationship. Even in friendships, this individual is often emotionally distant from close individuals.

Many professionals in the field of psychology, including Beverly James, have determined that the adult who struggles with dismissive-avoidant attachment disorder were children whose parents demonstrated significant emotional neglect and/or were very dismissive of the child's needs and emotions.

Another subtype of avoidant attachment pattern is the fearful-avoidant attachment style. The individual who struggles with the fearful-avoidant attachment disorder may long for closeness and emotional intimacy, but have such strong fear with emotional intimacy that they reject their partner. There is significant internal conflict within this individual's brain pertaining to wanting intimacy and not wanting intimacy.

Fearful-Avoidant Attachment Disorder is a combination of the preoccupied attachment disorder of not believing one is lovable and the dismissive attachment pattern of not trusting others and not valuing intimacy. This mindset is also rooted in childhood. It is formed from inconsistent parenting, cold parenting or parents who do not take their children's emotions seriously or take their children's needs and desires seriously.

We should be looking at insecure attachment typologies and other insecurities in our lives as not having a firm and steady foundation. Our foundation is our internal working model. It is where we operate and execute all other functions in our lives. When we have secure attachment, we operate from a mindset of security, confidence, stability, and a sense that we will be okay. When we operate out of an insecure attachment typology, we execute all other functions from a position of ambivalence, low self-esteem, and insecurity. We just finished discussing the various typologies of insecure attachment patterns.

Another significant component to examine in the creation of a well wired internal working model is parenting typologies. Diana Baumrind (1970) studied numerous parents in their behaviors, attitudes, and parenting practices and derived that there are four basic parenting typologies.

The four basic typologies are 1) Authoritative, 2) Authoritarian, 3) Permissive, and 4) Uninvolved. Amongst the four different parenting typologies ranges a wide range of attitudes, discipline practices, a parent's degree of sensitivity toward their child, and a parent's attitude toward their children and their children's success in academics and other aspects of their child's life.

We will discuss the Authoritarian Parenting Style first.

This is best described as parents who are low in emotional support toward their child, yet high in demandingness toward their children. These parents have the belief that they are always in charge in reference to their children. They also expect their children to be always obedient to their parents. The parents' attitude is basically: you are my child so you obey me without question.

One of the positive attributes is that children grow up in a highly structured household, with rules and consequences clearly stated. Generally speaking, children growing up in these environments become obedient, compliant, and proficient. However, many children growing up in the authoritarian environment become adults who have difficulty knowing what they are feeling or difficulty expressing their emotions.

This is because they have not been taught about emotions and have acquired the belief that emotions are not important. In addition, many of these children growing up in the authoritarian environment struggle with happiness, self-esteem, and social competence. When researchers studied parenting styles across cultures, they did discover that Asian children performed well amongst all traits, including happiness. We always need to examine parental motives for their actions and attitudes toward their children.

The next parenting typology that we will discuss is the Uninvolved Parent. The uninvolved parent is the parent who ranks very low in any form of emotional support or sensitivity to the child's needs. The uninvolved parent is also very low in demandingness or any form of expectations from the child. Many psychologists associate the uninvolved parent as being at minimum emotionally neglectful, if not physically neglectful as well.

Physical neglect refers to the child's basic needs, such as food, shelter, clothing, and safety, are lacking for the child's wellbeing. Emotional neglectful refers to the parent's sensitivity toward their child's needs, parental warmth toward their child, and taking care of the child's emotional needs.

Children who grow up with uninvolved parents often struggle with almost every aspect of life including struggling with trusting and respecting anyone in authority, such as teachers, principals, and eventually the police. The children who grow up in environments with uninvolved parents lack the built-in safety net, I discussed earlier that becomes wired in a child's internal working model whose parent created secure attachment for their child.

I also stated earlier that a built-in safety net creates the ability to take safe risks, the ability to create structure which leads to working efficiently, effectively, and with confidence. The child who grows up in the environment of neglect also struggles with self-esteem, lacks control, and lacks competence in their academics and other skills. This child is on his or her own emotionally. Children need and thrive on structure, including rules, discipline, and warm parental interaction.

Another parenting typology that also lacks structure for the child is the Permissive Parenting typology. The parent who utilizes the permissive parenting typology is more involved in their children's lives than the parent who utilizes the uninvolved parenting typology. Permissive Parenting is focused on providing high support and lacking providing structure, rules or boundaries for their children. However, one major negative attribute of permissive parenting is indulgence.

This indulgence plays a significant role in a child's life negatively. First, indulgence robs the child from having their built-in safety net created. Therefore, the child is far less likely to explore their environment, far less likely to take healthy risks, and far less likely to reach their academic potential. Remember, children and adults alike thrive on structure. Structure creates the built-in safety net. Structure also creates boundaries. A lack of structure creates a lack of boundaries, which then can lead to narcissism and arrogance believing they can do whatever.

This narcissistic attitude of (I can do whatever) leads to a total lack of understanding and respect towards authority.

This starts in the child's life with his or her parents, then leads to his/her teachers, and then to the police. Obviously, this is not a good thing. Parents who operate out of the permissive parenting typology might have the attitude that they are teaching their children independence, when in fact these parents are neglecting their children.

Another common excuse by parents using the permissive parenting typology is (Well, they're children) revealing their defensiveness and arrogance that they know about children. This is far easier than acknowledging that they need to gain parenting skills and that they are lazy in their parenting by not creating boundaries and consequences for their children.

The child who was raised by parents who engaged in the permissive parenting typology can easily grow into a narcissistic adult who has no boundaries and no sensitivity towards others. This adult would have the attitude that everything they say and do is okay and others need to adjust themselves if they have a difficult time with the behavior of the narcissist.

There are numerous research studies that confirms Baumrind's (1970) research on parenting practices focused on two key components: Parental Support toward their children and Parental Demandingness (expectations) from their children. Parental Demandingness refers to the parent creating boundaries and consequences for the child. Parental Support towards their children refers to the amount of affection, acceptance, and warmth toward their child.

In my dissertation (Factors Associated with Parental Involvement in their Child's Education), I studied the effect of Baumrind's Parenting Typologies, Parental

Involvement, and Parents' Internal Attachment Patterns has upon Elementary School Children's Academic Success. I found that parental warmth, parental sensitivity toward their child, and a parents' attitude toward their child as well as a parents' attitude toward education that are key factors in their children's academic success. Parental Support and Parental Demandingness are key factors in almost all aspects of a child's success.

Baumrind's parenting typology, the Authoritative Parenting Style, shows that parental support is high and parental demandingness is also high. The Authoritative Parenting Typology shows that children whose parents utilize the authoritative parenting typology have higher self-esteem, demonstrates a higher level of competence, take more healthy risks, are happier, and more successful than other children.

When parents create a positive internal working model for their child in the first year of life, then the child will not become a sociopath. Now what about the child's second and third years of their lives? Earlier, I discussed the significance of parents creating limits and boundaries for their children. We also discussed how parents, through the process of setting limits and boundaries with their children, assist in imprinting an internal safety net. This built-in safety net impacts the child's success in exploring their environment and enhance their academic success and success in life.

I designed the above diagram to demonstrate the correlations between the different parenting typologies and the different attachment patterns. The manner in which we have been parented is imperative in designing, creating, and wiring our internal working models. The adults, children grow up and become is rooted in childhood. Yes, it is the adult's responsibility to determine the life that they want to live and they need to choose whether they want to heal their childhood wounds and to work toward a healthier, happier life.

At the same time, parents need to recognize the large degree of responsibility God has granted every parent. A parent's responsibility includes creating safety for their child, building trust, creating a built-in safety net by creating boundaries and consequences, and providing emotional and cognitive support to their child so their child can be successful academically and successful in life.

When parents create this emotional and cognitive environment the parent has wired an internal working model for their child that manifests in secure attachment. Secure attachment exemplifies high self-esteem, confidence, inner peace, and academic success for that child's aptitude. When a child is wired with secure attachment, the child grows into a securely attached adult who is wired for high success in their life's plan that they choose to live.

The sad fact is most individuals are not wired with secure attachment. The majority of parents are not securely attached individuals. The combination of having some pattern of insecure attachment and challenges in parenting leads to creating some pattern of insecure attachment. When parents demonstrate ambivalence in their parenting or are totally insensitive to their children's emotions or insensitive to their children's needs, then the parent is wiring into their child a disorganized insecure attachment pattern in their child.

When parents demonstrate an uninvolved parenting style or are neglecting their child's needs; the parent is wiring into their child an avoidant or dismissive insecure attachment pattern. Parents who are strong in discipline but demonstrate coldness, such as authoritarian parenting, wires into their child preoccupied (anxious-ambivalent) insecure attachment pattern. When parents demonstrate severe neglect that neglectful parent wires into their child reactive attachment disorder. These neglectful actions of the parent correlate along with the etiology of each insecure attachment pattern.

As long as an individual is alive, there is hope to change. Change is possible at any age. The key is desiring change enough to motivate an individual to do the hard work that is necessary to become healed and live the life one has always desired and deserves to live.

Transformation for the parent requires a highly skilled therapist. The therapist should be an expert in several areas: developmental psychology, attachment theory and therapy, how parenting is learned during childhood, how to train parents in becoming highly skilled parents, how the parents' unresolved childhood issues affect their current life along with their parenting, and an expert in relationship work. Another vital aspect for the therapist is that the therapist has worked through his or her personal transformation. Transformation is a spiritual journey one chooses to walk, in spite of all the obstacles, in order to discover one's true self-identity, one's essence.

10

Attachment as a Sociological Disorder

First, let's discuss the connection of sociology and relationship. Sociology is the study of the development, structure, and functioning of human society. It is the study of social processes, including what societies throughout the world need to be functional, how individuals develop, interact with one another, and become successful societies or how they fail. The United \States has many cultures and cultures within cultures that produce societies.

The overlap of sociology and psychology is while psychology focuses on the development of individuals, sociology focuses on groups of individuals which make up societies. It is this reason why I am discussing the connection between attachment patterns within individuals and the impact that those attachment patterns within individuals impact society. In this chapter, I will discuss this question along with how society in America has changed due to the attachment patterns within individuals which become attachment patterns within society.

We will begin discussing the differences amongst different generations by beginning our conversation on this topic by discussing the greatest generation first. The greatest generation was formed through some of the most challenging times in our country.

These challenging times were preceded by the gay 1920's, a time of big bands, dancing night clubs, and an era of partying and living high. Then in October 1929, the worst financial event occurred, the stock market crashed, which led to the great depression of the 1930's.

During the great depression, many wealthy individuals committed suicide because they were financially wiped out. They lost everything that was important to them. The rest of the population struggled with not having any money or not making enough money or being out of work. This challenging period lasted a decade. Then Hitler invaded Poland in 1939, which manifested into World War II. It took the bombing of Pearl Harbor by the Japanese on December 7, 1941, for the United States to enter the war.

Americans worked together as a well-functioning society which won the war. Factories were building fighter jets from scratch to completion in seven hours. The men who flew those jets fully understood there was a strong possibility they would die that day by flying that jet. Women took up the slack and went to work by the thousands. There was a tremendous change in the culture with thousands of women leaving the home and going to work in the factories. In addition, the American public also sacrificed with numerous rations, doing without gasoline, without shoes, and many other basic daily items.

There was a team effort with one goal in mind, work toward peace and safety for the greater purpose of the group or in this case society. It was a period of time when the nation was united. Society, for the most part, acted as a unit. The United |States was not divided. The attitude was humble and the motto was we are in this together. No matter how small the job, everyone was focused on the major goal, which was much larger than anyone individual working toward the unified goal of a successful, safe, enjoyable country to live in. This is why this group of individuals is named the greatest generation.

The greatest generation went through a lot of Hell and yet came out on top. It was the last generation that would demonstrate diligence and perseverance in spite of several uphill battles. It set the stage for other generations to follow utilizing perseverance and diligence to move through problems and achieve.

One of the social mores/ attitudes that has changed significantly from the greatest generation is that during this period is that individuals appeared to know who they were and accepted their talents and their limitations. When people know who they are and are willing to accept that others might be very talented in the same areas that they have limitations.

The generations that followed the greatest generation had big shoes to fill. People evolve and therefore cultures and societies evolve. After the war had been won and Europe was on a long road of rebuilding, the United States was entering into their most prosperous period ever. The majority of the American population had money and financial security, which had been missing for a few decades.

Simultaneously, there were racial tensions between black Americans and white Americans. In addition,

Japanese Americans were going through a lot of prejudice, which started during World War II, starting with the bombing of Pearl Harbor. The federal government had placed thousands of Japanese American citizens into Japanese American Internment Camps.

There has always been an underlying prejudice and ranking system in the United States. The movie, Gangs of New York demonstrates this progression from the British in America being prejudiced against the Irish Americans, to the Irish |Americans having control of the majority of government jobs (police, fire personnel, telephone, utilities, political) toward the prejudice of Italian Americans, and onward and so forth. There has always been a competition of whose who according to ethnicity in the United States.

In spite of the competition amongst ethnicities, Americans also strove toward compliance and fitting in. It appeared that everyone wanted to be like everyone else. The old joke was all the houses looked alike; everyone dressed the same. No one took the time, during this era, to recognize conformity. In spite of the Joseph McCarthy era of looking for secret communists living and operating in the United States, the majority of Americans didn't realize that through attempting to have the same size and same shape house, similar type vehicle, and dressing where everyone looks like they belong are some of the same ways individuals in communist countries live.

The conformity of the 1950's entered into the early 1960's. The early 1960's was nicknamed the innocent age with the decade ending in the turbulent 60's. The 1960's were started with the youngest president, the United States ever had, John Fitzgerald Kennedy. We were in a race for space, simultaneously fighting in Vietnam, and simultaneously the racial tensions between black and white Americans were building.

With all of these events, a major change was underway. The majority of the population were young adults and voting age. There was a major political, psychological, emotional, and societal change going on and young individuals were leading it. The times they were changing, and this is more than just a song by Bob Dylan. The music through the decade was becoming more and more radical. The clothes were also becoming more and more radical and just very different than anything previously designed. The traditional lifestyle was radically being changed.

There was several very different events and lifestyles going on simultaneously. There was the radical hippy movement. There was the civil rights movement building lots of attention and lots of dedication from numerous individuals, in addition to Martin Luther King Junior. Then you had the war going on in Vietnam, where the majority of soldiers were 18 to 21 years of age. Another large and significant population was the college students and the war protests. In addition to all of these populations were the folks who just wanted to remain mainstream the best they could, to work a regular 9 to 5 job, be married, raise children or just live a life of mainstream America.

Let's examine the population whose mentality was I want to do things differently. I do not want to carry on the generational tradition of doing what my father did before me. This young generation was challenging everything that had been laid out previous to their generation. This generation was challenging the Jim Crow Laws of the South and were fighting for positive change, fighting to be treated equally in spite of skin color. Then there was the draft that every male when they turned eighteen years old had to register for the draft. It didn't matter what your beliefs were; it mattered that you were willing to fight for your country and be willing to die for your country, if necessary.

Individuals were questioning the rules. Who makes the rules? What is the basis of the rules? What was the purpose of the rules? One of the popular protest songs, (Eve of Destruction) had several profound lyrics, many lyrics demonstrated significant contradictions. One of those major significant contradictions was "you're old enough to kill but not for voting" It was the first time that young adults were in charge. It was also the first time the American people were so focused on change in numerous ways and simultaneously making major changes.

This was a generation that stood out. The generation of the 1960's can be compared to the greatest generation in that numerous significant events were happening in both eras. In addition, both the greatest generation and the generation of the 60's were experiencing great change that affected societal changes. These societal changes impacted future generations.

If we were to examine these very different generations from a parenting perspective; it probably would be safe to safe that the majority of the greatest generation were raised by parents utilizing Baumrind's authoritarian typology. While the parents who raised the 60's generation was most likely to fall more into the authoritative typology or the permissive parenting typology.

The authoritarian parenting typology is more likely to raise children who grow into adults that are compliant, rule followers, and more likely to follow in the footsteps of their parents. While parents who utilize the authoritative parenting typology are more likely to raise children who grow into adults who feel comfortable questioning authority, who analyze situations more before saying yes to something. These young adults will acquire further self-esteem than children raised by parents who utilize other parenting typologies. Children who were raised by parents who utilize the permissive parenting typology are more likely to grow into adults who are risk takers and do not analyze the possibility of consequences.

The 1960's started with a slow boil and worked up to a raging fire on many fronts then slowly simmered into the 1970's, the me generation. Political events had quieted down significantly during this decade. Some of the clothing and hair styles, especially for men, had drifted over into the 70's. The music was changing, ending the decade with a brief period of disco music, and leisure suits. The mentality was changing with a more self-focused mind frame.

In the summer 1972, President Richard Nixon's administration broke into the Democratic headquarters, the Watergate building. This was an event that caught

American's attention. The Vietnam War and now Watergate had really broken the trust of Americans toward the government and its officials. The American people were losing hope as well as trust in the US government. Americans were beginning to separate from the crowds and focus more on autonomy.

The search for self, began in the 60's with the hippy movement. It was still common during the 70's era for individuals to search for self-identity. Things mellowed out, including the sexual revolution. It was an era of individuation. The marijuana phenomenon started in the 60's and carried into the 70's. But as with most things, individuals are always looking for more, whether it is more money, different style clothes, more radical music, or a better drug. In spite of all the hallucinogenic drugs of the 60's, it was pot that became the most popular in the 70's. With the soldiers returning from Vietnam, marijuana came with them. The United \States pentagon ended our participation in Vietnam in 1973.

Many of the vets were suffering with PTSD. There are several major reasons why this generation suffered more from PTSD than vets from previous wars, including World War II. One of the major contributors of PTSD was the majority of these soldiers were 18 to 21 years of age. This is a very young age for individuals to be involved in war, especially coming from the United States.

Another very significant component was that in Vietnam, you never knew for sure who your enemy was and who was on our side. In addition, there was numerous hand to hand combat in Vietnam. While a lot of \World War II was fought in the air or with tanks. There was a very different war strategy in Vietnam and Vietnam had very different terrain than America or any of the countries in Europe.

This was a very different war on very different terrain and with a very mixed set of support from the American public. The majority of the soldiers were drafted and did not want to be there. They were in a place that some didn't even know where Vietnam is located, did not understand the culture, did not understand the reasons why we were involved and was on their own when it came to emotional survival.

Now in the 70's many individuals sought the comfort of marijuana to keep some type of inner peace. The resignation of Richard Nixon left Gerald Ford in the presidency. The American people were so upset and feeling helpless. The one place Americans felt that they had some power and control were in the voting booth. Jimmy Carter became president. The federal government protested and refused to attend the Olympics. In addition, the Iranian crisis came about in 1979, where Iranian college students belonging to the Muslim Students of the Imam Khomeini Line had occupied the United States Embassy in Tehran and took 52 American diplomats hostage for 444 consecutive days.

The culmination of the significant influx of marijuana, disco music versus rock, leisure suits, the Iranian crisis, extremely high inflation, gas prices that had risen exponentially, quarter-mile long gasoline lines, and even gas rationing was the culmination of the 1970's. This was an era that was an era of transition. The times they were a changing once again. There were significant differences between the 1950's, the innocent age into the turbulent 60's and then the mistrust and self-absorption of the 1970's.

The self-absorption of the 70's transitioned into the 1980's 'Greed is Good" mentality for the decade of the 80's. This was a decade of the wealthy becoming wealthier. This decade fit the movie, 'Wall Street', which showed a Hollywood version of the high that inside traders received from trading and the high they received from cocaine and other drugs. We have been discussing the evolution which takes place from one decade onto the next and so on. Remember, the 70's was all about me and now that is increased to me and money.

This was a decade of Ronald Reagan, the oldest president we have had in office with promises of everyone receiving their share of the wealth and to back government out of everyone's life. Perhaps, Ronald Reagon was a rebel in the way that during his first inaugural speech, he stated "Government is not the solution. Government is the problem".

There was a further shift toward self-absorption, with attempts to get away from traditional roles, with attempts towards deeper liberty and even attempts towards freedom from government. Even the music was changing towards liberty and individualism. Hip Hop and Rap most definitely represent free expression of self. In addition, the music of the 80's had a new genre, electronic music made from synthesizers. The hairstyles and the clothes were changing once again.

The 1980's are known for greed, an era where individuals were focused on making as much money as possible as easily as possible, and a period of time for self-expression. This was an era with the many of the young adults having been raised by parents who utilized the permissive parenting typology. This is manifested in individuals who struggle with boundaries but seek opportunities for self-expression. These individuals seek opportunities for their next high, their next adrenalin rush.

This led to the 1990's, the era of the internet. The internet changed the way individuals would connect and communicate to each other forever. But, we didn't realize this in the 90's. In the 90's, we just thought it was cool that the world was interconnected through some mystery called the internet.

Communism had significantly diminished in the world with fewer countries upholding a communist government. The Soviet Union became \Russia. This era was the most prosperous time throughout the world. The music of the 1990's moved from the electronic sound of the 80's to a huge popularity of hip hop scene. In addition, there was grunge music, alternative rock and roll, gangster rap, punk rock, and further exploration of self-expression.

The 1990's was the era that started with the term of President Herbert Bush and the end of the Republican era and moved toward a huge difference in political power and beliefs with Bill Clinton in office. The biggest scandal and popular news was the affair of intern Monica Lewinski and the president of the United States. Monica Lewinski fulfilled her goal and made a huge name for herself and a great book deal. These two names and this affair was known all over the world.

Other big names that came out of the 1990's was Bill Gates, Microsoft, Kurt Cobain lead vocalist of Nirvana, Mel Gibson, Tom Cruise, Robin Williams, Julia Roberts, nd Tom Hanks. Michael Jordan, Michael Jackson, Celine

Dion, Robin Williams, Whitney Houston, and Tupac Shakur. These individuals made a huge name for themselves during the 1990's. The 1990's made these individuals very wealthy and famous.

The 1990's was a decade of prosperity for many individuals. Necessity was no longer the mother of invention. Instead, convenience, comfort, and the need for more became the mother of invention. The collection of the most toys became an incentive for success during this era. Storage units rose exponentially during the 1990's. This was the era of SUV's. An era of unnecessary large vehicles once again. Houses became huge during this era, not out of necessity, but out of show and see me. The entitlement of the 1990's became the philosophy of the 90's.

This was an era where individuals demanded respect and had attitudes that money ruled. Stock markets were skyrocketing. Individuals were living lifestyles that they dreamed about. The Clintons had established numerous positive programs. Bill Clinton's administration had: wiped out the federal deficit, had created the longest economic expansion in American history, created more than 22 million new jobs, created the highest home ownership in the nation, created the lowest unemployment in history, increased education standards, created the largest expansion of college education, created higher police resources, including cops walking the beat again, and created the most diverse cabinet in |American history. Wise Americans associate Lincoln, FDR, and Clinton as amongst the greatest of all presidents.

An era, the 1990's, of great prosperity, is when Americans were achieving their financial and academic goals more than any other era. The biggest transition from the 1990's into the new century was Y2K phenomenon. The internet was only a decade old and computer software is written in binary (0's and 1's). The concern was how would computer software handle transitioning from 99 to 00.

Many individuals were concerned that it would be a disaster and would wipe out all financial documents and all other documentation that involved utilizing the year 2000. Zero, 0, represents off; while one, 1, represents on in digital code. There was concern that the year 2000 would be mixed up with the year 1900 and would crash the system. Many companies were prepared to handle this issue for their usage. Other organizations had received data and dates like January 2000 as 1/1/19100 or 1/1/100. The problem was eventually resolved without major disasters.

The first 10 years of the Millenium were interesting times. Internet usage and popularity had risen exponentially. This decade started out with prosperity and ended with The Great Recession, according to Obama. I strongly believe it was actually a depression that had blanketed the United States in the latter years of the first decade. Numerous stores were closing and even entire malls in some cities had closed during this period of time. There were numerous foreclosures in every neighborhood in the United States. Jewelry was being sold at 70% off. Unemployment had more than doubled during the latter half of the 2000's. There was over 14-million individuals out of work. Houses were being abandoned, businesses closed, nonprofits closing, individuals lost thousands of dollars in their pensions and stock portfolios.

These factors are much more manifestations of a depression than a recession. A recession manifests in higher prices, an increase in unemployment, and a decrease in housing prices. Many individuals suffered from an upside-down mortgage, where individuals owed more on their house than what the house is worth. This created many individuals to just abandon their houses. In addition, many individuals suffered from losing thousands in their retirement funds and investments. There was a worldwide financial crisis.

It took close to a decade to recover from these financial disasters, another significant sign that we were in the depth of a depression. There was once again an attitude of despair, disappointment, not trusting others, definitely not trusting government. This was also a decade of significant loss of trust and an imperative change in mind-set of Americans toward the world and the viewpoints of others.

The events that occurred on September 11, 2001 will forever be remembered. FDR gave a very famous speech on December 7, 1941, stating that the world will always remember December 7, 1941 because of the bombing of Pearl Harbor. September 11, 2001 will be a date that will always be remembered due to the Taliban using commercial airlines to bomb the World Trade Center in New York City, the Pentagon Building in Washington DC, and an alleged failed attack on the Capitol building in Washington DC. The names al Qaeda and Osama bin-Laden will be remembered for decades. The leader and group responsible for the 9-11 attacks.

These events of 9-11 changed the world forever. Starting with all air traffic, except for emergency transportation, being grounded for two days. Almost immediately, there was a vast difference in security measures and those security measures for planes and trains became even stricter over time. George W Bush was president during this time. The United |States had invaded

Afghanistan almost immediately after al Qaeda attacked the United States. In March, 2003, the United States entered into Iraq. We were now dividing military troops into two separate but simultaneous wars that really stretched our military.

In addition to the two wars in Afghanistan and Iraq, financial crisis and significant stock frauds were also taking place simultaneously. The most popular and perhaps dramatic stock fraud and financial crisis was the Enron crisis. Enron was an electricity, natural gas, communications, and paper company. Enron was listed by Fortune magazine as 'America's Most Innovative Company' for six consecutive years. Enron had revenues of $101 billion and had over 20,000 employees. Then it went bankrupt.

In the interim between the days of a very prosperous corporation to a stock market crash to a major cover-up and the largest fraudulent situation in the history of the United States. The scandal involved inflated stock prices. Some individuals, mainly executives, became wealthy. While the majority lost thousands of dollars in their investment in Enron stock. In the summer 2000 Enron's stock prices went from $90 per share to less than a dollar in a matter of months.

The first decade of the millennium were trying times for most Americans. With two wars in the middle east, a culture and geographical terrain that Americans have not mastered, vital financial fraudulent crisis, foreclosures in almost every neighborhood, many businesses closing their doors for good, unemployment more than doubled and a depression going on during the second half of this decade; it was a decade of survival. Individuals were working hard to just get by.

Parenting typologies were changing during this generation. There were fewer parents utilizing the authoritarian parenting typology. Unfortunately, there have always been parents who have neglected their children either physically or emotionally. Therefore, there will always be parents who utilize the uninvolved parenting typology.

Divorce and single parents became the largest population of parents during the 2000's. With these family dynamics, it is also common to have more parents utilize the permissive parenting typology. However, there were many more parents who were taking parent education classes. Therefore, there were also many more parents who utilize the authoritative parenting typology.

Parenting typologies affect attachment patterns. I discussed earlier in the book and displayed in my attachment pattern diagram, the correlations between parenting typologies and attachment patterns. Unfortunately, there will always be child maltreatment.

Therefore, there will also be insecure attachment patterns (reactive attachment disorder, anxious-ambivalent, avoidant attachment, and disorganized attachment pattern). In addition, attachment patterns are passed down from one generation through parenting practices being repeated from one generation to the next generation. With more parents working on themselves as well as working on their relationships with their children; the authoritative parenting typology is more utilized and therefore, there are more children growing up with secure attachment.

Parenting typologies affect families and family mindsets make up societal norms and societal mind-sets. The decade from 2010 to 2020 was a decade recovering from all the traumatic events of the first decade of the millennium and working toward a transition of easier times and different times.

President Obama became president in 2009 and led the second decade of the millennium to 2017. This decade became a period of economic growth and stability in the stock market and financial investments. The housing market was rising once again. In several states, individuals were making money and the housing market became a seller's market, People were working again, with the lowest unemployment rates in several years. Americans felt stable again, at least financially.

In spite of financial stability, several American cultural groups were involved in attempting to change things for the better. One-percenters became a term. Approximately a thousand individuals marched and protested on Wall Street expressing the significant inequality of finances amongst the American population. This was known as Occupy Wallstreet. American CEO's earn in a week the same amount that many blue collar workers earn in a year. While in Japan, there is only a 10% difference in salaries between maintenance workers and CEO's. America is a land of opportunity for the select few.

Another group of individuals inspired by the Civil Rights Movement, the Black Power Movement, and Occupy Wallstreet created the Black Lives Matter was started by three black females. These three black females were motivated by the acquittal of George Zimmerman, who shot and killed an unarmed black teen, Trayvon Martin. As the decade continued, the Black Lives Matter grew in popularity and in power.

Another significant cultural separation and strive for identity was The United Kingdom. Brexit was where the United Kingdom voted to leave the European Union. This was mostly led by Boris Johnson, the Prime Minister at the time.

In spite of financial stability for many, this decade was also a period of time with a lot of unease. In addition, to Brexit, Occupy Wall Street, and the Black Lives Matter movements progressing, there were also significant terrorist attacks occurring.

There were several mass school shootings. Perhaps, the most known school shooting was Columbine on April 20, 1999. Since then, there have unfortunately been hundreds of school shootings, many of which occurred in the 2010's. There were devastating acts of school shootings at Sandy Hook Elementary School in Newtown, Connecticut; Marjory Stoneman |Douglas High School in Parland, Florida, and dozens of others. One of the most traumatic experiences any individual can experience is the death of their child.

In addition to school shootings, other public and devastating mass shootings took place during this decade. The most known tragic events were a movie theatre in Aurora, Colorado; a historic black church in Charleston,

South Carolina; and a country music festival in Las Vegas. There were more American adults purchasing guns more than anytime in American history since the days of the old West.

There were also terrorist acts such as the Boston Marathon bombing. On April 15, 2013, two bombs were detonated by Dzhokhar and Tamerlan Tsamaev. Their reasoning was the wars in Iraq and Afghanistan. Three people were killed, 17 individuals lost their limbs, and hundreds of individuals were injured. There are significant horrific tragedies that leave innocent individuals with overwhelming undeserved pain because of total assholes who were significantly misguided. When individuals are striving for power and control with misguided information, people get seriously hurt.

This leads me to discuss a very unlikely person to even run for presidency, actually won the 2016 presidential candidacy. That individual is Donald Trump. Many psychologists classify Donald Trump as the most narcissistic president in the history of the United States. Before the 2016 election, the American people heard another new name, Bernie Sanders, a Vermont Senator.

Americans knew the name, Hillary Clinton, wife of former President Bill Clinton in the 1990's.

To win an election is not much different than to win popularity in high school. You tell the people what they want to hear. Donald Trump had a lot of money to do what he pleased. A lot of money went into the coaching of Donald Trump for president. Behind the scenes is a team that conducts research on the mind frame of the voters. Trump mastered the language of the voters out there most likely to vote republican and to vote for Trump.

Donald Trump mastered the language of his people. His team studied and fully understood who his followers would be. Over 63% of Trump's followers are uneducated. This term has been confused amongst some individuals. The pure definition of being educated infers that the individual has a minimum of a bachelor's degree.

In addition to being uneducated, many of these individuals were angry about how their lives turned out.

Many individuals felt cheated or felt left behind and that they did not have a voice. Donald Trump spoke their language and spoke to them. Trump's words fed their minds, their anger, and they fed the ballot box for Trump. President Trump became the third president to be impeached. Trump has the personality that people will either love him or can't stand him.

There was more division in the country between the Trumpers and those who had a different mind-set. When I taught college during these years, I made a point to tell my students that the most distinctive trait I witnessed amongst this new generation was their ability to accept others. This was very different than the way people treated each other when I was growing up and even in my twenties. During my youth and my twenties, there were racial fights, fights against gays and lesbians and there were even fights between those who liked disco and those who wanted old fashioned rock and roll.

During the decade of the twenty-tens, many individuals were learning about acceptance. It was during this decade that homosexual marriage became legal in many countries. The legalization of homosexual marriages poured over into the LGBTQ individuals receiving more positive attention and acceptance. It was also during this decade that Aspergers disorder became integrated into the autism spectrum. Many individuals were becoming sensitive to the differences of others.

In addition to becoming more sensitive to the differences of individuals, there was also more attention paid to victims' rights. During this decade a powerful group of women started the me-too movement in 2006 but exploded into popularity and power in the courtroom through New York Time Magazine's article in 2017 on the rumors of his numerous sexual harassment and sexual assault accusations. Many women felt that they had a voice due to the me-too movement.

This was an intense decade mixed with groups standing for victims, groups standing for change, individuals who wanted a chance of returning back to the good ole days through Make America Great Again, and other individuals who took on their mission to hurt, kill, and make a name for themselves.

The stock market was back up, property values increased significantly, and people were working. However, it didn't really matter when their happiness is concerned. The research shows that 1) few people are actually happy and 2) these outside influencers, attributes, and assets did not seem to manifest into happiness.

The year 2020 came in like a lamb, but very quickly became like a lion. With a worldwide pandemic, the year 2020 became a talking piece throughout the entire world. It has remained a talking piece, what did you do during 2020? With President Trump in office during this pandemic, there was as much division in the country as there was during the 1960's.

There was division between Trumpers and almost everyone else. There was division between those who were adamant about wearing masks and those who thought it completely unnecessary to wear masks. There was division between those who took Covid seriously and those who saw Covid as some type of scam.

It was also a period of division between those who believed in isolation and those who ignored the rules. Many individuals have difficulty thinking autonomously. Most individuals find the camp/tribe that they feel most comfortable with and follow the rules of that particular tribe. Part of living according to the rules of your particular tribe is to criticize the rules of the tribes in opposition to your set of beliefs.

In addition to all the different types of divisions taking place in this powerful year; there was also a lot of isolation. Corporations were forced to have employees work from home. Schools were closed, while children went to school online at home. Colleges no longer held classes in the classroom. Instead, college students took their classes online in their home environments.

Many businesses closed during this time because people did not shop. There were strict rules of having a limited number of individuals in any given place, work, stores, shops, school, or churches. This was an extremely tough period of time for many individuals attempting to make a living. There were many individuals unemployed. Many businesses closed their doors forever.

Hospitals were filled. Doctors and nurses were overwhelmed with the number of patients they were receiving. Many doctors and nurses were exhausted and experiencing vicarious traumatization from the number of individuals who died from Covid during this year. This was a trying period of time for many individuals in a variety of ways.

Anxiety rose exponentially during this single year. Many individuals were scared of dying. Many individuals were scared of their loved ones dying. Many individuals were scared of becoming ill with Covid. Plastering all these stories all over the television and radio was very harmful. It significantly enhanced the degree of fear amongst the American people. Many individuals were reactive out of their fears and anxiety.

Then several months later, George Floyd and Derek Chauvin became household names. During an arrest of George Floyd in Minneapolis, Minnesota, police officer

Derek knelt on Floyd's neck for 9 minutes, causing George Floyd to suffocate and die. This hit the news like a roaring bon-fire. Soon, after the news there were protests and riots in numerous cities across the country, with the mission that Black lives matter. There is a series of black individuals who have died during interactions with white police officers.

So, now in addition to the worldwide pandemic and thousands of individuals filled with fear of acquiring Covid and dying, there was enhanced fear of being hurt by groups of angry individuals. Trust had significantly plummeted amongst the American people. There was chaos and mayhem everywhere you turned. The mental state of the American people was mistrust, fear, anxiety, and panic.

The two most anxiety provoking events of the millennium was 9-11 and the Pandemic. 2020 was a year of stress, isolation, anxiety, depression, and tension. Many individuals thought Trump was the wrong person to be leading us through one of the most challenging times the world has experienced, the pandemic. Others thought Trump was correct in his thinking and followed the words and beliefs of Trump.

This led to strong division amongst the American people during the presidential election of 2020. Many individuals predicted and expected the close election that the 2020 presidential election was. However, no one predicted that it would take several days to tally the votes and determine the winner of the presidency for the next four years.

President Donald Trump became the only president in the history of the United States that conjured up false allegations that the election was rigged. In addition, President Trump became the only president in the history of the United States that had extreme difficulty conceding the election, doing the right and mature thing. All of this led to the insurrection that occurred on January 6, 2021.

All of these events led to further division in the nation. We have been living during an era where everyone wants to be treated equal and everyone wants their uniqueness recognized. According to the book of revelations, we are definitely living in the end times. We are living in an era where people are definitely lovers of themselves.

Vehicles have evolved once again. In our latest era, individuals are buying vehicles that are unnecessarily large vehicles hogging parking spaces. There are thousands of individuals buying and driving trucks just for the sake of feeling important. They are not really utilizing their trucks as trucks. The beds of their trucks are hardly touched. They just want to feel their power over something big and makes them sound and look important.

The American people have evolved into a group of individuals demanding to be viewed as special, as important, as awesome. And at the same time, everyone wants equality. This era has been a period of time when individuals have shown acceptance of others.

This has also been a period of time for self-absorption. Individuals drive much more aggressively than they ever have. There are many more drivers who swerve in and out of lanes just because they believe they are important and that they have the right to do so. In my day, individuals paid attention to the rule that the speed of your vehicle should reciprocate with the amount of space between vehicles. Now everyone, including police officers drive onto each individual's bumper. Everyone is in a hurry to go nowhere because they want to believe they are important.

Other ways that individuals attempt to strut their importance is having no regard toward others. People block doorways, hallways, aisles, and even sidewalks because of that attitude that no one else matters and they are ultimately important and it works for them. Then, you have the individuals who have no shame and are comfortable with being loud even in public places. If it works for me, no one else matters, it is all about me is the most recent motto and mission statement for many Americans. Mother Teresa clearly stated, "America is the poorest country in the world, spiritually".

A lot of this comes from Baumrind's parenting typology of permissive parenting. With the permissive typology, parents do a great job at providing physical and emotional support. However, with this parenting typology, parents have grave difficulty with setting boundaries and addressing their children's misbehavior.

Some of the challenge is the high divorce rate, each of the child's parents are concerned with their limited time with their child and is also concerned with looking as the bad parent through the child's eyes. So, this parent becomes more lenient and focuses on forming a positive relationship with their child. The parent is concerned about losing time with their child through disciplining their child. In addition, the divorced or co-parent is concerned with their co-parent having a 'better relationship' with their child. So, the parent competes for their child's attention and love through attempts of becoming friends with their child and/or through making their child happy.

These traits affect the children. The children's behavior affect the schools and level of education in the country. The children's behavior also affects society. According to the Pew Research Center, approximately 19 million children live in a single-parent household. These children and parents live in very stressful households. Many of these single parent families are living in poverty. Living in poverty creates many additional stressors, living in dangerous neighborhoods, access to gangs, poor schools, and living with far less opportunities.

Two more tragic statistics about American children are that 50% of children come from divorced parents. A second statistic is 40% of American children are growing up without their fathers. When you culminate all of these components and stressors of the parent, from financial stress to time constraints, to low energy, and limited resources; parents are on survival mode most of the time they are with their children. This mostly impacts the child in that children are not receiving discipline. The good news is that the majority of children are receiving their parents' love and physical and emotional support.

However, the other side of this parenting coin is that without discipline on a consistent basis, children grow into adults who have difficulty with pain and disappointment. As I stated earlier, we are currently living in a generation of self-absorption, narcissism, and self-importance. The challenge is when everyone attempts to be important, then no one and nothing is important, except themselves.

When that happens, empathy is significantly diminished. In addition, customer service is significantly diminished. Loneliness is significantly increased amongst the population. Suicide and suicide ideation is significantly increased. Individuals feel alone in the world and as if they don't matter. Violence is also significantly increased from those who have had enough and are ready to lash out and make a name for themselves.

This period of time is vastly different than the period of time of the greatest generation. Things have changed drastically. The mind-set of the American people has changed drastically. In the book of revelations, God warns us that near the ending times, people will become lovers of self. I believe we are in the beginning chapter of the ending times. No one knows the exact time when the very last days are here. At the same time, God warns us to pay attention to the signs of the last days.

Behavior is often predictable. And we can predict the future behaviors and mindsets of the population by paying attention to the behaviors of current times. The most common parenting typology used in a particular generation always leads to the next generation's mind-set, attitude and beliefs. The purpose of studying history and archaeology is to understand the patterns of behavior which can then be used to predict future behaviors. We have choices over our behaviors, our words, and our attitudes and beliefs.

www.ingramcontent.com/pod-product-compliance
Lightning Source LLC
LaVergne TN
LVHW021803060526
838201LV00058B/3216